Tolley's
Client and Adviser Guide
to
Hotels

by
Jonathan Pryor
Smith & Williamson

Tolley Publishing Company Limited
 A United News & Media publication

Published by
Tolley Publishing Company Limited
Tolley House
2 Addiscombe Road
Croydon Surrey CR9 5AF England
0181-686 9141

Printed and Bound in Great Britain by
Hobbs the Printers, Southampton

ISBN 0 85459 997–5

Acknowledgements

The *Tolley's Client and Adviser Guide to Hotels* was written by experts at three professional firms.

The author wishes to thank colleagues at Smith & Williamson, Chartered Accountants for their contributions, including Angus Sim for his overall assistance; Andrew Bond for Chapter 5, the Audit of Hotels; Kevin Stopps and John Voyez for Chapter 7, Tax Issues; and Bob Empson for Chapter 12, Marketing.

Chapter 3, Legal and Regulatory Background, was written by Pamela Thomsen-Hall, Michael A Stubbs and Simon R Wethered of Alsop Wilkinson.

Chapter 4, Property Valuation and Chapter 8, Business Rates were written by Jonathan Flowith of Grimley, International Property Advisers. Jonathan would like to thank the colleagues who helped him in the preparation of elements of the book, specifically Christopher Lloyd, Martin Farr, Colin Sharp, Roland Morgan and Paul Watson.

Preface

The hotel industry is one of the most competitive. As we at Forte know only too well guests demand a high quality service and innovative products. However, a successful hotel company also needs high quality and innovative professional advice from its internal financial experts and its external professional advisers. This book has a dual role – it provides industry specific advice to those working in the finance departments of hotel companies and provides professionals called on to advise them with a database of relevant accounting, property, tax and legal information. We welcome it as a useful information source for those working in and for the industry.

Mrs Olga Polizzi
Managing Director, Building and Design
Forte plc

Contents

Contents

Contents

Chapter 1

Introduction

Scope and aims of this book

1.1   The hotel industry has witnessed turbulent times during the last decade, starting with the 1980s boom and followed, perhaps inevitably, by the 1990s recession. Those hotels that kept their heads through this period and did not lose sight of the business basics have survived and are now able to flourish. Many others got carried away and more often than not their businesses have failed.

This book is not a response to what went wrong. The recent past has illustrated that the hotel industry attracts all sorts of people into it, many of whom are unprepared for its demands. Furthermore, it is not a simple business with which anyone with no experience can get involved and expect to flourish. It is in fact very complex and very competitive.

This book attempts to provide a reasonably comprehensive, but not exhaustive, guide to the key areas affecting the industry. Relevant areas are brought together in a concise form. As such it will be useful to those in management as well as to investors. It is also aimed at consultants and other professionals who provide services to the industry.

The chapters of the book which deal with areas such as property valuation, law and taxation are a guide to the key aspect of these subjects. In particular the law relating to hotels, guest houses and restaurants is both substantial and complex. Chapter 3 is designed to draw the reader's attention to those particular areas of law which may be of specific relevance but it is not intended as a substitute for independent professional advice which, it is recommended, should be sought in all circumstances.

Chapter 2

The Market Place

Development of the market

2.1   The hotel sector represents one of the UK's largest industrial sectors and it plays an important role not just as a major employer, but also as a wealth creator via its contribution to invisible exports. The sector's turnover is estimated at over £6 billion. During the late 1980s employment in the industry grew by over 20 per cent to peak at over 303,100 in 1990. Employment in the industry has since declined to 287,000 in 1993. The period of the early 1990s has seen the industry contract due to the effects of first the impact of the Gulf War on tourism and then the recession. However, its growth is forecast to resume in the coming years, for example the demand for managerial staff in the industry is expected to grow by 2 per cent per annum during the 1990s.

Market size

2.2   There are some 42,000 registered hotels with over 860,000 bedspaces in the UK, according to the British Tourist Authority. These estimates include guest houses, motels, holiday camps, hostels and other units providing furnished accommodation, most of which have fewer than 10 rooms, as illustrated by Table 1 on page 3. If these smaller establishments are stripped out it is a reasonable estimate that there are around 18,000 to 19,000 hotels in the UK.

Market structure

2.3   A clear pattern exists in the industry of a pyramid structure with a large base of small units. Units with turnover of less than £500,000 account for 85.6 per cent of all hotels. In contrast only 0.9 per cent of hotels have a turnover of over £5 million, as Table 3 on page 4 illustrates.

Classification

2.4   The larger categories of hotels have been classified by groups such as the AA and RAC. The AA, for example, classifies hotels according to its well-known one to five star system. However, when a hotel changes hands, its classification expires because the AA will wish to reassess the hotel under its

Table 1: Pie chart showing the UK hotel sector by category of hotel

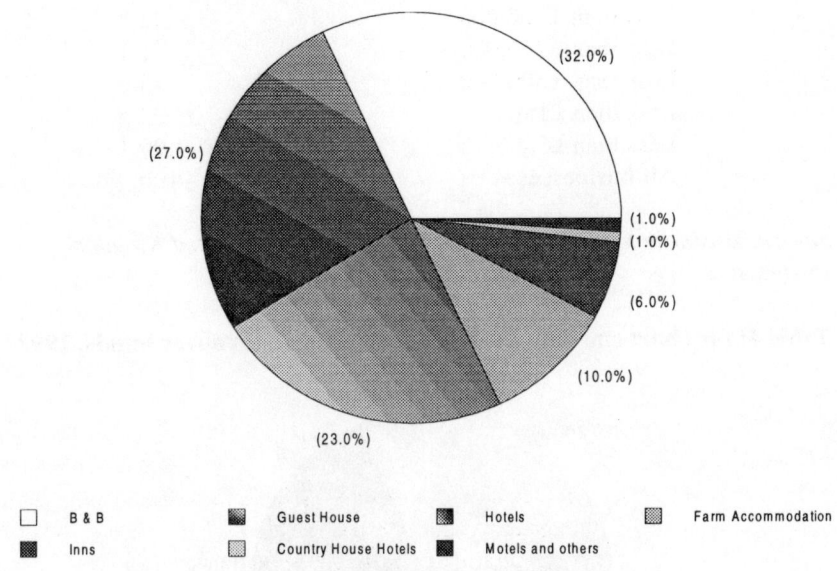

Source: Grimley and British Tourist Authority – October 1994

Table 2: Percentage of hotel sector by category of hotel

Type	%
B&B	32
Guest Houses	27
Hotels	23
Farm Accommodation	10
Inns	6
Country House Hotels	1
Motels and Others	1

new management. As a result, a significant risk involved in purchasing a hotel is the possibility that its classification will be downgraded following acquisition.

The star system is augmented by further categories, including 'AA Lodges', 'Country House Hotels' and the red star merit system. Five stars represent the highest possible award, while to be awarded one star only certain minimum standards must be achieved. Most hotels are 'unclassified', usually because they are too small to warrant classification. Table 5 overleaf illustrates the distribution of hotel bedrooms according to the AA's classification system.

2.4   *The Market Place*

Table 3: Percentage of hotels in turnover bands per annum, 1993

Less than £50,000	20.2
Less than £100,000	43.8
Less than £250,000	71.1
Less than £500,000	85.6
Less than £1m	93.5
Less than £5m	99.1
All businesses	100.0

Source: Business Monitor PA1003 – Size analyses of United Kingdom Businessess

Table 4: Pie chart showing the UK hotel sector in turnover bands, 1993

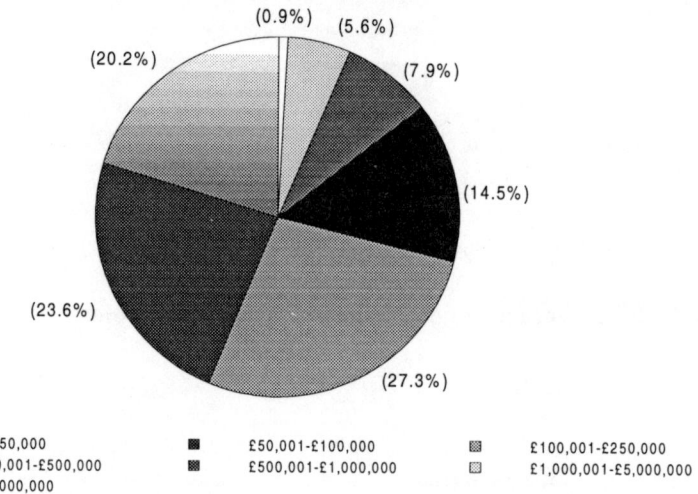

▨	£0-£50,000	■	£50,001-£100,000	▨	£100,001-£250,000
■	£250,001-£500,000	▨	£500,001-£1,000,000	▨	£1,000,001-£5,000,000
☐	>£5,000,000				

Table 5: Distribution of bedrooms according to AA classification

AA classification	Bedrooms
5 star	7,797
4 star	43,042
3 star	115,642
2 star	38,997
1 star	12,116
AA Lodge	2,004
Unclassified	273,620
Total	**493,218**

Source: HCTC, 1992

Customer categories

2.5   The structure of the industry has developed according to the different types of customer that frequent hotels of different standards and locations.
The most significant types of customer are tourists and businessmen. At the
bottom end of the market, characterised by the 'unclassified' types of establishment, tourists, holiday-makers and weekenders are the most significant
customer. Further up the market the business travellers become increasingly
important, especially in the three star category. Research carried out by Horwath
Consulting, the results of which are shown as Table 6, confirms this pattern.
Their survey of 293 hotels found that 41.6 per cent of guests in 1991 were
business travellers, compared with 19 per cent for holiday tourists (although
the tourist market had suffered due to the Gulf War and the recession). While
the market share of both the business traveller and the tourist has shrunk over
the five years to 1991, that of the conference delegate has risen sharply from
5.1 per cent in 1987 to 17.9 per cent in 1991. The business traveller and
conference delegate now represent up to 60 per cent of the market, whilst
tourists will typically represent around 28 to 30 per cent which was near the
average for tourists in the years prior to the particularly bad year of 1991. It
should be noted that this survey took its sample from hotels that are larger
than average and so there is likely to be some over-emphasis of the importance of the commercial sector customers at the expense of the tourist sector if
one were to apply it to the whole hotel population.

Table 6: Customer categories

	1987 %	1988 %	1989 %	1990 %	1991 %
Business traveller	49.2	49.1	39.9	42.0	41.6
Holiday maker	32.8	31.7	28.3	28.2	19.0
Conference/seminar delegate	5.1	5.0	13.0	15.0	17.9
Other	12.9	14.2	18.8	14.9	20.3
Total	**100.0**	**100.0**	**100.0**	**100.0**	**100.0**

Source: Horwath Consulting

The figures in Table 6 give an overall picture of the key types of customer in
the UK hotel trade, particularly for the larger hotels. It should be noted, however, that these figures will vary significantly according to location and time
of year. For instance, the London market is far more dependent on the business
market than the Scottish sector, while some of the traditional holiday resorts
such as Bournemouth have augmented their usual summer holiday trade with
autumn conference trade.

2.6   The Market Place

Table 7: Barchart showing customer categories

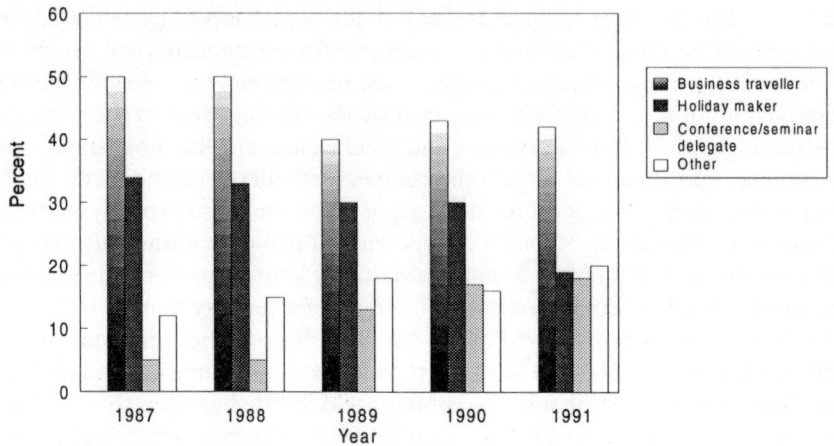

Since 1991 the pattern has remained virtually unchanged according to the 1994 Key Note Report.

Guest origin

2.6   The origin of hotel guests is dominated by domestic demand with UK guests accounting for some 60 per cent of the market. In terms of sales overseas guests are often more important due to their greater spending power. However, this tends to depend on their country of origin and upon the type of hotel in question. The dominance of the domestic customer is chiefly due to the importance of the domestic business market. Table 8 illustrates the origin of guests.

Table 8: Origin of guests

| | 1987 | 1988 | 1989 | 1990 | 1991 |
	%	%	%	%	%
UK	61.8	62.2	57.0	63.9	59.9
US and Canada	19.1	15.0	17.1	15.8	15.5
Other Europe	11.1	12.6	13.9	10.9	13.3
Japan	2.4	3.5	3.4	4.6	4.1
Middle East	2.1	2.2	2.4	1.6	1.5
Australia	1.1	1.1	1.5	1.6	1.4
Other Africa	0.5	0.9	1.0	0.6	1.0
Other Asia	1.1	1.6	2.4	0.6	1.1
Latin America	0.5	0.7	0.9	0.2	1.8
North Africa	0.3	0.2	0.4	0.2	0.4
Total	**100.0**	**100.0**	**100.0**	**100.0**	**100.0**

Source: Horwath Consulting

6

Table 9: Barchart showing the origin of guests

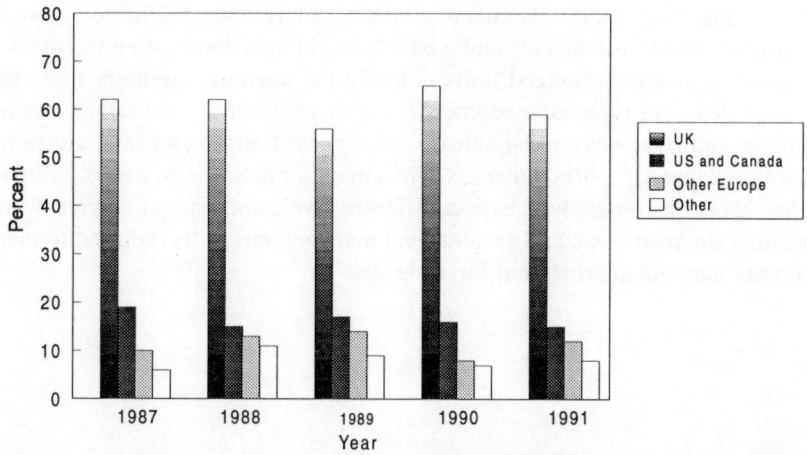

The bottom half of the hotel industry is dominated by owner-occupiers of small hotels and guest houses. The upper half is dominated by groups of companies, lead by Forte which is over twice as big as its nearest competitor. The trend over recent years has been the emergence of hotel groups to a dominant position in the industry. This trend is likely to continue and is driven by the increasingly effective manner in which companies are now projecting their brands to attract and keep corporate guests.

Table 10: Largest hotel companies in the UK ranked by number of bedrooms, 1994

Rank	Company	Rooms	Hotels
1	Forte	30,362	344
2	Mount Charlotte Thistle Hotels	14,288	112
3	Queens Moat Houses	10,332	100
4	Hilton UK	8,440	40
5	Swallow Hotels	4,379	35
6	Accor UK	4,338	29
7	Holiday Inn Worldwide	4,210	24
8	Stakis Hotels	4,056	33
9	Country Club Hotel Group	4,000	78
10	Jarvis Hotels	3,680	46
Total		**88,085**	**841**

Source: AA's 'Hotels and Restaurants in Britian and Ireland, 1994'

Summary

2.7 The hotel market is characterised by a large number of operators at the smaller end of the market and a handful of chains dominating the market for large- and medium-sized units. Clearly the various operators meet the needs of different types of customer. The larger city hotels are dependent on business and oversees tourist sales, whilst guest houses and inns are more reliant on domestic tourist business. The key point to this is that each of these outlets serve customers who expect different levels and type of service. Consequently the resources, and systems and management skills required to meet customer demand are different for all levels.

Chapter 3

Legal and Regulatory Background

Definitions

3.1 An hotel is an expression defined by statute as follows:

'the expression "hotel" means an establishment held out by the proprietor as offering food, drink and, if so required, sleeping accommodation, without special contract, to any traveller presenting himself who appears able and willing to pay a reasonable sum for the services and facilities provided and who is in a fit state to be received'.

[*Hotel Proprietors Act 1956, s 1(3)*].

To fall within the definition it is not necessary that there should be any form of name or sign advertising the hotel, nor does it have to have alcoholic refreshments for sale. The reference to 'travellers' is intended to differentiate hotels from lodgings or boarding houses, and would not exclude a local resident coming in for refreshment.

In most circumstances the law regards an hotel and an inn as synonymous (see 3.24 below) but distinguishes them from public houses (which do not provide sleeping accommodation if requested), 'taverns' which principally offer wines and other liquors for sale, coffee houses and lodging or boarding houses.

Trading vehicles

3.2 The first fundamental question to be considered from a legal point of view in establishing an hotel is the type of legal 'person' that will own and/or operate the hotel.

The three principal alternatives are:

(*a*)   a limited liability company;

(*b*)   a sole trader; and

(*c*)   a partnership.

3.3 Legal and Regulatory Background

The limited liability company

3.3   The attraction of this alternative is that it offers protection from personal liability, subject to certain exceptions, e.g. personal liability for wrongful trading (*Insolvency Act 1986, s 214*) so that if the business were to fail for any reason, the creditors would have recourse only to the assets of the company, and not to the shareholders, directors, or employees of the company. In practice, particularly if the company is incorporated with only a nominal share capital, third parties (such as landlords, leasing companies and banks) may only be willing to transact business with the company if its liabilities and obligations are guaranteed personally by some or all of the directors and shareholders.

A number of company incorporation agents specialise in the provision of 'off-the-shelf companies' so that for a fee a company with the power and authority to own and operate an hotel can be purchased, duly incorporated under the *Companies Acts 1985* to *1989* and registered at Companies House. Every company has a Memorandum of Association which sets out what it is established to do and its powers (e.g. to buy land, borrow money, issue debentures and do all such other things as may be necessary to enable it to operate); it also crucially provides that the liability of the members (i.e. its shareholders) is limited. The limit, in the case of companies limited by shares, is to the paid up share capital of the company and in the case of a company limited by guarantee to the amount (usually nominal) provided for in the Memorandum. However, for an ordinary trading company, a company limited by shares will be the appropriate vehicle, so that the shareholders can pay themselves dividends out of the company's distributable profits.

Every company also has Articles of Association, which regulate the manner in which it will operate, e.g. the meetings of shareholdings and directors, the appointment and retirement of directors, the powers of the directors and the transfer of shares. There is a statutory standard form (Table A set out in the *Schedule* to *SI 1985 No 805*) which in straightforward cases (see 3.6 below) will be adopted subject to minor, simplifying amendments drafted by the Company Incorporation Agents.

The benefit of limited liability brings with it, however, certain important statutory duties and additional costs. Returns have to be made to Companies House and (subject to certain exceptions in the case of small companies (*Companies Act 1985, s 246*)) a directors report and audited accounts prepared each year. Breach of these requirements can entail fines and there may be auditors fees to be paid. The tax implications of conducting any hotel business through a company, rather than as a private individual or in a partnership, must also be carefully considered before deciding on whether this is an appropriate vehicle.

10

Sole trader

3.4   Particularly if the business is to be conducted in a modest way, it may be appropriate for an individual to conduct the business as a sole trader, so that he is personally liable on all contracts entered into (and for all claims that may be made by third parties) up to the full amount of their personal assets. Appropriate insurance can alleviate some of the risks of liability to third parties but otherwise a sole trader will be personally liable to, e.g. landlords from whom any premises are leased and suppliers of equipment, food and drink and for the employment of staff. If the relevant turnover limits, currently £45,000 are reached, there will also be the personal liability to account to Customs & Excise for all and any value added tax properly payable. Again, specific tax advice should be taken on the implications of operating an hotel as a sole trader.

Partnership

3.5   Partnership is defined (*Partnership Act 1890, s 1*) as 'the relation which subsists between persons carrying on a business in common with a view of profit'. Persons, for these purposes can be private individuals and also limited liability companies. A partnership may be a limited partnership where one or more partners undertake to be liable for all the debts and obligations of the firm and others (called limited partners) are liable only up to the amount contributed by them. [*Limited Partnership Act 1907, s 4*].

Crucially, every act of a partner in the usual course of the firm's business commits all the other partners, and each of the partners is jointly liable, and severally also in Scotland, for the debts and obligations of the firm while he is a partner. It is for this reason that partners owe each other a duty to act in the utmost good faith.

Any partnership should be regulated by a partnership deed or agreement, prepared and negotiated with the help of competent legal advice. This document defines not only the nature of the partnership's business and the name under which it will trade, but all matters relating to the management and financing of the firm's business and the manner in which profits or losses are to be shared. The admission and retirement of partners will also be dealt with, as well as any restrictive covenants that may bind partners as to activities they may or may not engage in during or after termination of the partnership. Partnership taxation is a complex topic and will need proper consideration before this vehicle is chosen in preference to any other.

A hotel business may be run using a permutation of any of these alternatives so, for example, a private individual or partnership may own or lease the premises from which the business is carried on while the trade itself is conducted through a limited liability company.

3.6 *Legal and Regulatory Background*

The joint venture company

3.6   A further vehicle for the establishment of an hotel business, which is often appropriate in the larger projects and deserves more detailed treatment, is the joint venture company. At its heart will be a company limited by shares in which the participants in the project will be the shareholders. One party may be providing the land, another carrying out the building or refurbishment, and a third operating the hotel for the joint venture company.

The mutual rights and obligations of the participants will be carefully and thoroughly defined in a joint venture agreement entered into by the parties, as well as by the Articles of Association of the company. Both sets of documents are necessary because the Articles filed at Companies House are public documents available to public scrutiny, so parties may prefer to regulate commercially sensitive areas by a private agreement, which will usually provide that (with necessary exceptions) its terms are to be kept confidential.

The Articles in a joint venture company

3.7   These will need to be drafted specifically to suit each project, but such Articles have a number of common features.

(*a*)   Each participant will be allotted a different class of shares, in proportion to their interest in the joint venture, so that typically the company will have 'A' Shares, 'B' Shares and 'C' Shares (if there are three participants) but it may also have Preference Shares (giving a right to a fixed dividend) and any one or more of the many variants of the Preference Share.

(*b*)   Each class of shareholder will be entitled to appoint (and equally importantly remove) one or more directors, depending on the proportions in which the participants' respective interests in the project are to be reflected in voting rights at meetings of the directors. This is necessary because, as a matter of company law (*Companies Act 1985, s 303*) a simple majority of the shareholders of a company may by ordinary resolution remove a director at any time. Plainly it would be unsatisfactory in a joint venture if two of the shareholders could, by exercising their voting rights, remove the director(s) appointed by the third participant. However, it has been decided (*Bushell v Faith AC 1099*) that if the voting rights attaching to shares are suitably loaded in favour of a director threatened with removal, the powers of a majority of the shareholders can effectively be nullified in this respect. The different classes of shares contain such weighted voting rights.

(*c*)   The right to transfer shares will be restricted and there will be pre-emption rights so that shares cannot be transferred to any potential new participant without having first been offered to the existing shareholders.

(*d*)   The regulation of directors' meetings to ensure a balance between each participant's right to have a say, and his capacity to damage the company's business by staying away from meetings.

(*e*)   Frequently there will be a number of matters on which the unanimous approval of each class of shareholder or director will be required e.g. a change in the company's business, entering into guarantees or unusual or onerous contracts, borrowings in excess of certain limits and so on.

The joint venture agreement

3.8   In many respects the joint venture agreement is a cross between a partnership agreement and the Articles of a company, for it regulates the carrying on of a business together with a view to deriving a profit from the company by a number of parties. However, the distinction between a partnership agreement and a joint venture agreement is that a joint venture agreement will specifically provide that nothing in it is intended to create a partnership between the parties, to avoid the sharing of liabilities that partnership involves. Other matters provided for in detail in the joint venture agreement will include:

(*a*)   arrangements for the establishment of the joint venture company;

(*b*)   detailed provisions on the business of the company;

(*c*)   the respective parties' obligations as to the financing of the company to ensure the project can be seen through (the question of whether guarantees have to be provided to banks for borrowings by the company is a delicate issue here);

(*d*)   any confidential arrangements relating to board meetings and the manner in which decisions on certain critical issues are arrived at;

(*e*)   taxation matters;

(*f*)   dividend policy; and

(*g*)   the duration of the agreement. This will need to deal with the resolution of any deadlock that may arise, particularly if there are only two participants, and can entail complex option arrangements so that one party can buy the other out. These are sometimes known as 'the Mexican Shoot-out' or 'Russian Roulette' clauses.

Management Contract

3.9   Many hotels, particularly those forming part of larger chains, are not operated using any of the structures outlined above, but using a Management Agreement. Typically one party – an investment company or wealthy individual – will own the land and buildings comprising the hotel but will appoint professional managers to operate the hotel. The terms of the arrangement will be set out in detail in the Management Contract.

These contracts provide in minute detail for every aspect of operating an hotel, starting with the design, decor, furnishing and equipping of it, the name under which it is to be operated and the arrangements for opening if it is newly built or refurbished.

The term of the contract will be of crucial importance to the operator, for having invested time and money in establishing the hotel and perhaps having paid a premium to the owner to secure the contract the operator will be loathe to see the hotel operated by a competitor for some considerable period. Typically, there will be a minimum period of several years followed by a right for the operator to renew for two or more further periods, provided there is no breach of the contract.

Other aspects requiring careful negotiations are:

(*a*)   control over cash and access to bank accounts;

(*b*)   involvement by the owner in the business plan;

(*c*)   the choice of senior staff;

(*d*)   the rate of management fee charged;

(*e*)   the proportion of gross operating profit retained by the operator; and

(*f*)   the definition of gross operating profit.

The Agreement will also deal with such practical matters as alterations, repairs and refurbishment, insurance responsibility and what happens if the hotel is damaged or destroyed. The circumstances in which an agreemnt can be terminated for breach or insolvency will be carefully spelled out, as will the basis upon which either party can assign it to a third party.

Planning status

3.10   Broadly speaking, it is likely that a building proposed to be used as a hotel is either a hotel already, used for another purpose or not yet constructed. Clearly where a property is not yet built, planning permission will be required for its proposed construction and use. However, in the case of an existing building, careful consideration needs to be given to planning status and whether planning permission needs to be obtained to authorise the proposed change of use.

For the purposes of planning legislation, development which requires planning permission includes both operational development (building, engineering, mining or other operations) and the making of a material change of use of any buildings or other land.

Certain changes of use are, however, exempt from the requirements to obtain specific planning permission under the provisions of the *Town and Country*

Planning (Use Classes) Order 1987 (SI 1987 No 764). Under Part C Class CI of the *Order* changes of use to and from boarding or guest houses and hotels are permitted. (The Government has recently amended this class which originally included hostels. The effect of this is that planning permission will be required to change from a hostel to a hotel use or vice versa.) (See 4.12 below.) In all other instances, however, where a material change of use is proposed planning permission will be required. For example, where it is proposed to change an existing residential dwelling, public house or nursing home to hotel use.

If it is apparent that the property has been used as a hotel by the previous owners or operators, but searches reveal that no planning permission exists for this use, the use may none the less be lawful if, for example, it has continued for an unbroken period of at least ten years prior to the date of the acquisition. The local planning authority may then be barred from taking enforcement action against the existing use. In this instance, it is worth giving consideration to making an application to the local planning authority for a certificate of lawful use or development in respect of the use. If that certificate is granted the lawfulness of the use is then conclusively presumed.

In all cases, where there is no satisfactory evidence of planning permission for hotel use of the building, it is worth considering whether to make the contract for the acquisition or lease conditional upon planning permission satisfactory to the purchaser being obtained. Similar clauses may be appropriate if a certificate of lawful use or development is to be applied for.

Alterations and maintenance

3.11   Even if a purchaser or a lessee satisfies himself in relation to the planning status of the property, it is likely that he will want to undertake internal alterations or create additional accommodation or floorspace. These may also require specific planning permission as they may fall within the definition of operational development, or involve a material change of use of part of the property. Certain types of operation are, however, specifically exempted from the definition of development by virtue of the *Town and Country Planning (General Development Order) 1988 (SI 1988 No 1813)*.

In the case of a building which is listed under the *Planning (Listed Buildings and Conservation Areas) Act 1990* internal alterations, improvements or maintenance works may well require listed building consent even if they do not require planning permission. Exterior alterations most certainly will.

Where it is proposed merely to change the use of part of the existing building, e.g. for use as a conference centre, then even if no operational development such as to require planning permission is proposed, it is likely that planning permission for a change of use of part of the existing building will be required.

If, however, it can be shown that this proposed use is merely ancillary to the hotel use, i.e. it does not exist as a separate unit or use in its own right, then planning permission may not be required.

There are rights of appeal to the Secretary of State for the Environment against a refusal, conditional grant, or non-determination of both applications for planning permission and listed building consent.

It is also important to remember the extensive powers of enforcement in the hands of the local planning authority when unauthorised works or changes of use are carried out without planning permission (or listed building consent when it is required).

In all instances, where alterations or new buildings are proposed, building regulation consent may also be required whether or not specific planning permission is needed.

Registration with tourist boards

3.12   Four tourist boards have been established in Great Britain (*Development of Tourism Act 1969*):

(*a*)   the British Tourist Authority;

(*b*)   the English Tourist Board;

(*c*)   the Scottish Tourist Board; and

(*d*)   the Welsh Tourist Board.

These boards run registers in relation to hotels and other establishments at which sleeping accommodation is provided by way of trade or business. Registration is not compulsory, and subject to certain constraints, no formal consents are necessary to establish and operate a hotel. However, if a hotel is registered with a tourist board, it will be necessary, having provided the required information, to pay the relevant fees, display the appropriate signs, submit to random inspections, and comply with a Code of Conduct and minimum standards, failing which the boards have power to impose a fine.

The licensing system in relation to hotels, guest houses and restaurants

3.13   Liquor licensing law is both substantial and complex. The principal governing legislation is the *Licensing Act 1964* (the annotated version runs to 215 pages). This section is intended to draw the reader's attention to topics to be borne in mind when approaching this subject and in particular for the purpose of instructing the reader's solicitors in taking the following matters forward or in consulting the court directly. Reference must be made to the relevant sections of the *Licensing Act 1964* to ensure proper compliance with the *Act's* procedural requirements and provisions.

Liquor licensing – the general prohibition

3.14   It is an offence if any person:

'sells or exposes for sale by retail any intoxicating liquor without holding a Justices' Licence ... authorising ... the sale of that liquor or when holding a Justices' Licence ... sells or exposes for sale by retail any intoxicating liquor except at the place for which that licence authorises ... the sale of that liquor'.

[*Licensing Act 1964, s 160*].

Intoxicating liquor includes spirits, wine, beer, cider (including perry) and other fermented, distilled or spiritous liquor. [*Licensing Act 1964, s 201*].

Licensing Justices' General Policy Statement

3.15   Many Magistrates' Courts issue, free of charge, a written statement of their requirements concerning liquor licensing applications. As a first step, a copy of this should be obtained from the Magistrates' Court where the relevant premises are situated.

Grant of licences

3.16   A Justices' Licence is granted by a panel of Licensing Justices who hold licensing sessions periodically throughout the year during which they may grant, remove, transfer and renew Justices' Licences. There are two forms of Justices' Licence namely on-licences (including restaurant licences, residential licences and combined restaurant and residential licences) and off-licences.

(*a*)   On-licences authorise the sale of intoxicating liquor either on or off the licensed premises but may be subject to a condition prohibiting the sale of intoxicating liquor for consumption off the premises. On-licences may authorise the sale of:

   (i)   intoxicating liquor of all descriptions;

   (ii) beer, cider and wine only;

   (iii) beer and cider only;

   (iv) cider only; and

   (v)   wine only.

[*Licensing Act 1964, s 1(3)(a)*].

(*b*)   Off-licences permit the sale by retail of intoxicating liquor for consumption off the premises and take two forms authorising the sale of the following:

(A)   intoxicating liquor of all descriptions; or

(B)   beer, cider and wine only.

[*Licensing Act 1964, s 1(3)(b)*].

Applications for grant, removal and transfer of a Justices' Licence

3.17   Applications are made by giving notice strictly in accordance with the procedural rules laid down in *Licensing Act 1964, 2 Sch* to the Clerk to the Licensing Justices, the Chief Officer of Police, the Local Authority, the Parish Council and the Community Council if there is any such council in the relevant area and to the Fire Authority in the case of a new licence or removal, not less than 21 days before the date fixed for the Licensing Sessions. Except in the case of a transfer, a similar notice should be placed in a newspaper circulating in the relevant area, not more than 28 days and not less than 14 days before the Licensing Sessions and a similar notice should be displayed on the premises not more than 28 days before the Licensing Sessions for a period of 7 days.

A plan will need to be deposited in respect of an application for a new On-Licence, or for an ordinary removal, which should outline the proposed licensed areas and indicate which area is to be a dry area and comply with any General Policy Statement issued by the Justices. An application for removal of a licence is done in the same way, save that notice must also be given to the registered owner of the premises, and to the licensee (unless he is also the applicant).

In respect of an application for a transfer, for example on change of management at hotel or restaurant premises, notice must also be given to the licensee but there is no requirement to give notice to the fire authority. For a transfer, there is no requirement for a notice to be placed on the premises or in a local newspaper and a deposit of a plan with the Clerk to the Licensing Justices is not required.

In some cases the appropriate application should be for a provisional grant of the Justices Licence sought, and reference should be made to *Licensing Act 1964, 1 Sch* for the specific procedural rules applicable to such an application.

Restaurant licences and residential licences and combined restaurant and residential licences (Part IV licences)

3.18   This section refers to on-licences and their use in hotels, restaurants and guest houses. These are known as Part IV licences. On an application for the grant, transfer or removal of a licence falling into this category, the Licensing Justices shall not refuse the application except as specified in the *1964 Act* provided, in particular, that the applicant is of full age and a fit and proper person to hold the licence; that the premises are suitably adapted and convenient for the purposes of the application and, where relevant, have appropriate sitting accommodation; that during the previous 12 months the licensed premises have not been ill-conducted or the applicant has not breached the requirements of the *1964 Act*; that the premises are not habitually used by persons under the age of 18 not accompanied by others of full age who pay for them and provided also for restaurant only or residential and restaurant licences, the provision of table meals, to which the consumption of intoxicating liquor is ancillary, is substantial.

(*a*)   Restaurant licence – A restaurant licence is one which falls within the definition of the *Licensing Act 1964, s 94(1)* in that the premises are:

    (i)   structurally adapted and bona fide used or intended to be used for the purposes of habitually providing the customary main meal at midday or in the evening, or both, for the accommodation of persons frequenting the premises; and

    (ii)   is subject to the condition that intoxicating liquor shall not be sold or supplied on the premises otherwise than to persons taking table meals there and for consumption by such a person as an ancillary to his meal.

(*b*)   Residential licence – A residential licence is one which falls into the category as defined by *Licensing Act 1964, s 94(2)* in that the premises are:

    (A)   'bona fide used or intention to be used for the purpose of habitually providing for reward board and lodging, including breakfast and one other at least of the customary main meals; and

    (B)   is subject to the condition that intoxicating liquor shall not be sold or supplied on the premises otherwise than to persons residing there or their private friends, bona fide entertained by them at their own expense and for consumption by such a person or his private friend so entertained by him either on the premises or with a meal supplied at but to be consumed off the premises'.

(*c*)   Residential and restaurant licence – A residential and restaurant licence is a combination of both of the above, in that the premises fall within the definitions of *s 94(1)(2)*. A condition is attached that the intoxicating liquor is not to be sold or supplied other than as permitted by the conditions of a restaurant licence or by those of a residential licence.

It is an implied condition that on premises to which a Part IV licence applies other suitable beverages, for example tea, coffee and water are to be equally available for consumption with or ancillary to meals served on the licence premises. In the case of a residential licence there must also be adequate seating facilities in the hotel in an area which is not used for sleeping or for the service of food and in which there will be no supply of intoxicating liquor. Such a room has become known as a 'dry room' and it is usually a condition of a restaurant and residential licence that such a room is made available. The licence may be granted without such a condition if the Licensing Justices consider in their discretion that there are sufficient reasons for not imposing it.

The conditions imposed on Part IV licences, once attached, cannot be varied or revoked and are usually imposed where Licensing Justices believe that a full on-licence would not be justified by the needs of the district and that they could be appropriately applied to an applicant who was operating an existing hotel or restaurant or was to adapt the premises to such trade. An application for a restaurant and residential licence may be refused if service of intoxicating liquor was to be performed by the residents or guests themselves on a self-service basis.

Undertakings and conditions

3.19   In addition to those conditions which are imposed on a Part IV licence, the Licensing Justices may require certain undertakings to be given or conditions to be attached generally to the licence. Whilst undertakings are common with off-licences, it is more usual to attach a condition rather than an undertaking to an on-licence. There are two categories of conditions; the first being those which are imposed on the grant of a new licence, e.g. a restriction as to the sale or consumption in certain parts of the premises, and which may not be removed or varied once imposed. The second category of condition may be imposed on grant, renewal or transfer, and these may be revoked or varied at a later stage. Examples of such conditions are as follows:

(*a*)   six-day licences which exclude sale of intoxicating liquors on Sundays;

(*b*)   early closing licences which shorten the period during which sale or supply of intoxicating liquor is permitted;

(*c*)   midday or evening meal licences; and

(*d*)   seasonal licences which restrict the sale of intoxicating liquor during permitted hours to specific times of the year.

Permitted hours

3.20   It is recommended that, notwithstanding the following comments, all licensees check carefully with their local Licensing Court the permitted hours which operate in their area for their type of establishment. At particular times of the year, it may be necessary to apply for permission to extend the hours of opening. It is an offence to sell or supply intoxicating liquor on licensed premises except during the permitted hours (*Licensing Act 1964, s 60* as amended by *Licensing Act 1988*) which are:

(a)   Monday to Saturday excluding Christmas Day and Good Friday between the hours of 11.00 am and 11.00 pm;

(b)   Sunday (other than Christmas Day) and Good Friday between the hours of 12.00 noon and 10.30 pm; and

(c)   Christmas Day, between the hours of 12.00 noon and 10.30 pm, with a break of four hours beginning at 3.00 pm.

Whilst this is the general rule, Licensing Justices can, where appropriate, vary such hours, except for the licensing hours which apply to Christmas Day. They may vary the hours so that they begin before 11.00 am, but not earlier than 10.00 am. There is a 'drinking up time' of 20 minutes at the end of the permitted hours which provides for a time in which intoxicating liquor which has been purchased during the permitted hours may be consumed (*Licensing Act 1964, s 63(i)(a)*) and a 30 minute 'drinking up time' for an intoxicating liquor which has been purchased during the permitted hours to be consumed ancillary to a meal. The drinking up periods also apply to permitted hours which have been extended by a general or special exemption, restaurant certificate, special hour certificate or an extended hour order.

(i)   *Restaurant licence*

(A)   Under the *Licensing Act 1964, ss 68, 96,* a restaurant certificate may be granted to enable intoxicating liquors to be served in conjunction with late meals. This extends the permitted hours by one hour to midnight and or alternatively, during the afternoon breaks on Christmas Day.

(B)   There is a further order available under the *Licensing Act 1964, s 70* which is available to some of the premises for which a supper hour certificate (now known as a 'restaurant certificate') is in place. This extends the permitted hours to a time not later than 1.00 am provided that the premises provide musical or other entertainment in addition to substantial refreshments. This is in order to facilitate the provision of entertainment such as cabarets as well as for entertainment which provides just music and dancing for the customers.

(ii)   *Residential licence* – The permitted hours of sale of intoxicating liquor for consumption in licensed premises are not applicable to those residing in the premises nor to their bona fide guests, provided that the resident pays for the guest drink. A similar exemption applies to those persons employed on licensed premises for the purposes of the business carried on by the licensee provided that the intoxicating liquor is supplied at the expense of the employer and the person is still working and the supply or consumption of the liquor ceases once the hours of employment have ended.

(iii)   *Restaurant and residential licences* – It will be appreciated that such a licence covers two categories of customers, those who are resident in a hotel or guest house and those who are merely dining there. Residents are entitled to the same exemptions to the permitted hours as would apply to a resident under a residential licence, that is, as discussed above, that there are no such restrictions for the resident or his bona fide guests entertained at his expense. In respect of those members of the public who are dining in the restaurant, they will, as with the restaurant licence, be entitled to benefit from the sale or supply of intoxicating liquor during the permitted hours and, subject to a supper hour certificate being in force for one hour after.

(iv)   *Opening during permitted hours* – It is not obligatory to open the licensed premises during the permitted hours (*Licensing Act 1964, s 90*). However, persistent closure of the premises during the permitted hours or any part may indicate to the Licensing Justices that such general permitted hours are not appropriate for those premises. The Licensing Justices may indicate that the premises are no longer servicing a need in the area and refuse to grant a renewal of the licence.

Altering licensed premises

3.21   In addition to any planning permissions which may be required from the planning authorities, in certain circumstances no alterations shall be made to premises for which a Justices' on-licence is in force, without the prior consent of the Licensing Justices. It should be noted that the Justices cannot give retrospective consent to alterations and that the penalties for making alterations not previously approved by the Justices can be severe. If the alterations provide increased drinking facilities in a public or common part of the premises; conceal from observation a public or common part of the premises used for drinking or; affect the communication between the public parts of the premises where intoxicating liquor is sold and the remainder of the premises or any street or any public way the consent of the Licensing Justices must be obtained (*Licensing Act 1964, s 20*). This would not affect any alterations which may be made to areas such as bedrooms and kitchens unless they may be within the area licensed. The consent of the Justices must be obtained unless the alterations are required by the local authority.

Children

3.22   It is an offence to allow children under the age of 14 into the bar area of a licensed premises during permitted hours (*Children and Young Persons*

Act 1933 and *Licensing Act 1964, s 168*). This excludes children under 14 who are the children of the licensee or who live in the premises but are not employed there or are purely passing through licensed premises as there is no other convenient way to pass.

It is an offence to sell intoxicating liquor to a person under 18 or to allow a person under 18 to drink such intoxicating liquor. A person under the age of 18 cannot be employed in a bar of a licensed premises when the bar is open for sale of intoxicating liquor. This does not include a bar which is in, for example, a dining annexe and which is only used for the sale or supply of intoxicating liquor when guests are taking meals at the tables.

Recent proposals for reforms of the law in relation to children have put forward the idea of what is known as a 'Children's Certificate' which would be enforced for the bar area. It would permit children into the bar area when they are accompanied by an adult. It is proposed that the Licensing Justices will have wide discretion as to whether such a Children's Certificate should be granted and they will take into account whether or not the premises constitute a suitable environment for children. They will also consider whether meals and beverages such as water and soft drinks are also available for sale in the premises.

Miscellaneous other licences

3.23

(*a*) Entertainment Licences (Music and Dancing Licences) – These licences are required for public music and dancing and are issued by the local authority and not the court. The local authority should be asked to supply an application form which will normally be accompanied by useful and helpful guidance notes. 'Public' is a term which can readily include what a layman might regard as a private function. In addition, some local authorities have adopted the *Private Places of Entertainment (Licensing) Act 1967*. Therefore checks should be made with the particular local authority whether the authority regards any proposed activity as private and not public if it is intended not to apply for a public entertainment licence. However, a public entertainment licence is necessary in most cases as a pre-condition for the grant of a special hour certificate.

(*b*) Special hours certificates – An extension of the permitted hours in licensed premises which are structurally adapted and bona fide used or intended to be used for the regular provision of music and dancing and substantial refreshment and to which the sale of intoxicating liquor is ancillary and for which an entertainment licence is in force is known as a special hours certificate. It extends the permitted hours for part or whole of the licensed premises not later than 2am on specified days of the week (3am in parts of London). [*Licensing Act 1964, s 77*]. 'Drinking up time' is increased to thirty minutes.

(c)   Supper hour certificates – An extension to the permitted hours at licensed premises with a dining room, structurally adapted and bona fide used by customers taking table meals to which the sale of intoxicating liquor is ancillary (*Licensing Act 1964, s 68*) can be granted by the Licensing Justices and are known as supper hour certificates. These extend the permitted hours by one hour from 11pm to midnight. 'Drinking up time' is also extended to 30 minutes. The supper hour certificate will only apply to the room which is set aside for the provision of meals, and not to the whole premises.

(d)   Gaming machine permits – It is not proposed to deal with legislation under the *Gaming Act 1968* because licensed premises such as hotels and guest houses generally do not qualify for a gaming licence or certificate. However, one particular area in which it may be relevant is gaming machine permits. This will relate to fruit machines and jackpot machines which by definition fall under *Gaming Act 1968, Part III*. A permit can be obtained under *section 34* which allows use of such machines within licensed premises. Such application is made by giving notice to the Clerk to the Licensing Committee only and by appearing before the Licensing Justices.

Other legal considerations

3.24   Whilst most business relationships entered into will be governed by the law of contract, breach of which could lead to a civil suit, there are also criminal law codes laid down by statute which, if not observed, could lead to prosecution, fines and imprisonment. It is therefore important for an hotelier to be fully aware of his legal obligations be they civil or criminal. These obligations are wide-ranging and it is not proposed to deal with all of them but to merely point the hotelier towards areas of particular concern.

Inns and private hotels

There is a difference between those establishments which are known as inns and those which are private hotels. It is easy to define the establishments which do not fit in to the category of inns (*Hotel Proprietors Act 1956*) in that they are generally establishments where the owner has a right to pick and choose the type of 'traveller' which attend the premises. The difference is important in that the innkeeper will have different liabilities to those of a proprietor of an establishment which is not an inn, e.g. the common law duty of an innkeeper is to provide every 'traveller' with reasonable refreshments at any time. An innkeeper also has statutory duties under the *Hotel Proprietors Act 1956*, e.g. in respect of a guest's luggage. In particular, an innkeeper has the right of lien over a guest's property, that is a right to keep the goods in lieu of payment of a bill for food and accommodation. This right extends to any traveller visiting the premises and would cover the situation where a guest taking a meal only refuses to pay a bill. Under the *Inn Keepers Act 1878*, the innkeeper also has a right of sale, subject to certain conditions, of those goods over which he is exercising a lien.

Occupiers liability

The occupier of the premises (the proprietor or hotelier) is responsible for the physical safety of all those persons who lawfully enter into the premises and owes a duty of care to them to provide that the premises are reasonably fit for the purposes for which they are provided (*Occupiers Liability Act 1957, s 2*). It is no defence to say that the negligence was a result of an employee's default. However, it could be a defence if the negligence was a result of a third party's default who had, for example, installed a bannister which collapsed, provided the proprietor or hotelier had done everything reasonably possible to ensure that the installation of the bannister had been done properly and securely. This duty of care extends beyond the building itself into the grounds of the hotel and includes all areas where guests normally visit.

Fire regulations

A proprietor of premises should be aware of regulations passed under the *Fire Precaution Act 1971* which relate to hotels, and the *Health and Safety at Work etc. Act 1974*, which relate to all places of work. Both cover the requirement for, amongst other things, fire certificates; adequate fire prevention; fighting equipment and adequate fire escapes. In particular, it is usually a requirement that self-closing doors and sprinklers are fitted to hotel premises prior to the granting of any such fire certificates. The hotelier will be fined and/or liable for imprisonment if he operates the premises without a fire certificate where one should be in place. Fire regulations must be considered in detail.

Insurance

Property and liability insurance should be taken out to cover every foreseeable eventuality. Property insurance should include, in particular, damage by fire, flood, storm and theft of both the hotelier's and the guests' property. High value items may need to be detailed on a separate policy. Liability insurance will be needed to protect against claims brought by guests or others who may injure themselves, and in respect of damage or loss to guests' property.

Relationship with guests

The contract

3.25 All relationships between the hotelier and the guests are governed by the basic rules of contract in that an offer is made and an acceptance is given which will bind the parties into the agreed terms of the contract which may be made in writing or orally. As well as the agreed terms of the contract, there will be terms which are implied by common law or statute, e.g. the implied term that all services be provided with reasonable care and skill. [*Supply of Goods and Services Act 1982, s 13*]. Such terms should be incorporated when the contract is made and cannot be imposed unilaterally after the guest has, for example, retired to his hotel room. It is important, therefore, to give guests as much information as possible concerning the services to be offered and the prices before they enter into a contract. Indeed, subject to certain exceptions, hotels must now display rates inclusive of VAT for their rooms in an obvious place, such as in the entrance hall or at the reception (*Tourism (Sleeping, Accommodation Price Display) Order 1977 (S1 1977 No 1877)*).

Breach by either party

If the guest who has reserved a room breaches the contract by failing to turn up a hotelier has a claim for breach of contract and may recover damages, based on actual loss. Likewise, if the hotelier fails to provide accommodation for the guest as agreed, the guest will be at liberty to sue for damages. In any event, whichever party does cancel the contract, each party is required to mitigate his loss so far as he is reasonably able.

Exemption clauses

An hotelier may try to escape liability by incorporating into the original contract an exemption clause which either excludes a remedy the guest may otherwise have or limits damages and imposes time limits for claims. These clauses must be incorporated into the contract either by the guest signing the contract or, if the contract was not signed, the exemption clause must be incorporated into the contract by taking reasonable steps to bring it to the guest's attention before the contract is made. Nearly all such exemption clauses are now governed by statute in that a party cannot exclude liability except in so far as it is reasonable to do so. [*Unfair Contract Terms Act 1977*]. Recently implemented European law also sets out many regulations which relate to oral and written consumer contracts which have not been individually negotiated. In particular there are provisions that require the use of clear language and deem any term unfair if contrary to the requirements of good faith, it causes a significant imbalance in the party's rights and obligations under the contract to the detriment of the consumer. If a term is unfair it will not be binding on the consumer. [*Unfair Terms in Consumer Contract Regulations 1994*].

Travel agents

The hotelier may wish to take particular care when dealing with travel agents, as it is important to clarify initially with the agent who will be responsible for payment. If it is the guest, the hotelier should obtain as much information about him as possible so that should he default, the hotelier has redress against the guest directly.

Misrepresentation

A guest may have a right of compensation which may take into account frustration and disappointment should the description of the hotel and its services not correspond to what is offered. It is a criminal offence to knowingly or recklessly make a statement which falsely describes any services or facilities on offer. [*Trade Descriptions Act 1968, s 14*]. Not only is there a civil obligation not to misrepresent the facilities on offer but also a statutory obligation under the *Trade Descriptions Act 1968* under which a prosecution could be brought.

Discrimination

It is unlawful for a person who provides facilities or services to the public (this includes hoteliers and similar catering establishments) to discriminate against a person on the grounds of colour, nationality, race or ethnic or national origins. [*Race Relations Act 1976, s 20(1)*]. It is also unlawful to discriminate against either men or women by virtue of their sex. For example, it is discriminatory where a bar owner refuses to allow women to drink at the bar when men are allowed to do so (*Gill v El Vino Co [1983] 1 All ER*).

Registration

A guest over the age of 16 must enter his name and nationality in the hotel register. Guests who are neither British nor Commonwealth citizens must also record their passport details, the date on which they are leaving and provide forwarding addresses. [*Immigration (Hotel Records) Order 1972 (SI 1972 No 1689)*]. The hotel register should be available for inspection by the police for a period of 12 months. Details in the book should be kept confidential and should not be produced other than to the police unless by way of court order.

Food and drink

Contractual and common law obligations

3.26   A further contractual relationship is created and governed by the rules discussed above when an hotelier agrees to supply food to a purchaser. There is an implied term that the food and goods sold in the course of a business be of satisfactory quality. [*Sale of Goods Act 1979, ss 13, 14; Sale and Supply of Goods Act 1994*]. There is also a common law duty of care to ensure that the goods produced, e.g. a meal, are reasonably safe for the purpose for which they were produced. In a famous example, a lady was bought a bottle of ginger beer, drank half and poured the remainder into her glass only to find a snail floating in it. Her resultant illness was as a result of the negligence of the manufacturer and she was able to claim damages for their breach of duty of care (*Donoghue v Stevenson [1932]*).

3.26 *Legal and Regulatory Background*

Statutory obligations

There is also criminal liability imposed by statute, the most notable being the *Food Act 1984* which creates an offence for a person to sell, offer or expose for sale, or to have in his possession for the purposes of sale, any food which is intended for human consumption, which is in fact unfit for that purpose.[*Food Act 1984, s 8*]. Possible defences to charges under the *Food Act 1984* are that all reasonable care was taken to prevent the offence being committed and that the purchaser was given full notice that the food was unfit for human consumption. It is also an offence to sell food which is not of the nature, substance or quality demanded (*Food Act 1984, s 2*) provided that the purchaser was not informed that he was getting something other than he had demanded, e.g. by way of notice on a wrapper or explanation on a menu. Other defences are that the offence was committed by another person; all reasonable care was taken to prevent its commission; a request is made that the person who actually committed the offence be prosecuted and that charges against the person originally prosecuted are dropped. [*Food Act 1984, s 100*]. Alternatively, there is a defence if the person prosecuted can show that he has bought food under a warranty which guaranteed its fitness for human consumption and that he had not tampered with it prior to selling it on. [*Food Act 1984, s 102*]. This may cover cases in which food is bought under a brand name.

Prices

An indication of the price, inclusive of VAT, of any food and drink available must be given unless, e.g. a meal is provided by way of a set menu in which case it is enough to display the price of the meal rather than identify the price of each item included. [T*he Price Marking (Food and Drink in Premises) Order 1979) (SI 1979 No 361)*]. It is also important to display any service charge or minimum price requirements prominently. Failure to display such prices, or to give an inaccurate price creates a criminal offence. [*Prices Act 1974; Consumer Protection Act 1987, s 20*].

Food Hygiene Regulations

These provide in particular for the conditions in which food should be handled, prepared and stored. Breach of the *Food Hygiene Regulations* may result in the premises being closed until the danger to public health has been removed to the satisfaction of the local authority. Breach of the *Food Act 1984* and its associated regulations can also result in fines or imprisonment.

Description of food

Any description applied to goods, the supply or offer to supply them which is materially false or misleading and which is in any way displayed so as to be associated with the goods in the mind of the purchaser, whether the statement is made orally or in writing, and which relates to the quality, quantity, composition, fitness for the purpose of safety of the goods offered creates a criminal offence. [*Trade Descriptions Act 1968, s 1*]. It would also be an offence to make such a false statement in relation to the price of goods. [*Trade Descriptions Act 1968, s 11; Consumer Protection Act 1987, s 20*]. Whilst there are defences available (*Trade Descriptions Act 1968, s 24*) any breach may lead to an order for payment by way of compensation.

The employer and the employee

3.27   A contract to provide services will not necessarily give rise to an employer/employee relationship. This only arises where the contract is a 'contract of service' not a 'contract for services'. The distinction is of great importance both in terms of employment protection legislation and tax treatment (see 7.2 below). The principal test for the existence of an employment relationship is the amount of control exercised by the employer over the manner in which work is carried out, though this test is not conclusive. Other factors taken into account include the right to delegate work, methods of payment envisaged, the contractual documents (if any) and the intention of the parties. The provisions of the contract must be consistent with a contract of employment and the employee's status as such. The label attached to the relationship by the parties is not itself conclusive so that simply describing a contract of employment as self-employment will not affect the underlying legal position.

Vicarious liability

An employer may be held vicariously liable for tortious acts carried out by his employees where those acts were carried out in the course of their employment even if the employer had strictly forbidden such acts unless he can show that he took reasonable steps to prevent such acts. The employee, however, remains primarily liable to the injured third party.

Contract terms

Certain terms are implied in an employment contract (oral or written) under common law, including the implied duty to pay the employee, for certain skilled workers not to withhold work unreasonably, to take reasonable care for the employee's safety and to preserve mutual trust and confidence. The implied duties of the employee are the duties of fidelity, the duty to account for monies and other benefits received and the duty of confidentiality. There are also certain statutory regulations which must be observed, in particular, the *Sex Discrimination Acts 1975* and *1986*, the *Race Relations Act 1976*, the *Equal Pay Act 1970*, the *Wages Act 1986*, the *Health and Safety at Work etc. Act 1974* and the *Employers' Liability (Compulsory Insurance) Act 1969* which requires employers to take out an approved insurance policy to cover all claims by employees in respect of work-related illness or physical injury.

Although an employment contract may be oral or written, it is always advisable to put the contract in writing to clarify the express terms of the contract and (if required) amplify implied terms. All employees must be provided with a written statement of the main contract terms not later than two months after they commence employment. (See *Employment Protection (Consdidation) Act 1978, SI* as amended.) The written statement must contain details of the identities of the parties, the date when the employment began, the date when the continuous period of employment began, remuneration, when paid, hours of work, holidays and holiday pay, sickness and sick pay, pension scheme (if any), periods of notice required to determine the contract, the job title, place of work, relevant collective agreements, grievance and disciplinary procedures, whether a contracting-out certificate is in force under the *Social Security and Pensions Act 1975* and, if the contract is for a fixed term or temporary, the date when it is due to expire.

Specific statutes may govern aspects of the employment contract including wages, conditions of employment, the provision of food, drink and accommodation and rest periods for those employees employed on the premises and permitted deductions from wages. An employer should also ensure that he complies with Inland Revenue requirements concerning deduction of income tax and National Insurance contributions from wages. Contribution tables in respect of these deductions can be obtained from the Inland Revenue and should be studied carefully before implementation. There may be exemptions for staff who are employed for less than a certain number of hours and for those staff who are under 16 years of age.

Termination of employment

If an employment contract is terminated in breach of its terms, the employee may have a contractual claim for damages for wrongful dismissal. An employee may also have a statutory claim for unfair dismissal (*Employment Protection (Consolidation) Act 1978, s 57*) or, in the case of redundancy, for a redundancy pay (*Employment Protection (Consolidation) Act 1978, s 81*) even if the dismissal was not wrongful. A contract may be terminated by agreement, effluxion of time, operation of law, or most commonly, by notice. Where there is an express notice period in the contract, the contract must be terminated in accordance with that express term or a claim for damages arises. Where there is none, a contract (other than for a fixed term) can be terminated by either party by giving reasonable notice. Certain statutory minimum periods of notice under which an employee who has been continuously employed for a period of at least one month but less than two years is entitled to at least one week's notice and thereafter one week's notice for each complete year worked to a maximum of twelve weeks. (See *Employment Protection (Consolidation) Act*

1978, s 49.) An employee who has been continuously employed for at least one month must give one week's notice of his intention to terminate. If the contract gives longer notice periods, these will prevail.

Wrongful dismissal

An employee claiming wrongful dismissal is entitled to damages to place him in the position that he would have been in had the contract been observed. For example, under a fixed-term contract he might be entitled to damages for the loss of the wages or salary for the remainder of a fixed term; or to recover lost wages or salary for the notice period. Such damages include compensation for lost benefits such as BUPA cover but in general not for loss of status or injured feelings. The employee has a legal duty to mitigate his loss and remuneration from other employment or state benefits received during the notice period reduce the damages awarded.

Redundancy

An employee dismissed by reason of redundancy with two years continuous service and who is between the ages of 18 and 65 is entitled to a statutory redundancy payment. [*Employment Protection (Consolidation) Act 1978, s 81, 4, 13* and *14 Schs*]. Dismissal is by reason of redundancy when the employer has ceased or intends to cease to carry on the business for the purposes for which the employee was employed or has ceased or intends to cease to carry on that business at the place where the employee was so employed, or the requirements for the employee to carry out work of a particular kind at the place where he was so employed have ceased, diminished or are expected to cease or diminish. If an employee is offered suitable alternative employment he may lose his right to a redundancy payment. [*Employment Protection (Consolidation) Act 1978, s 82*]. The employee is entitled to a four week statutory trial period to decide whether to accept the new offer of alternative employment. [*Employment Protection (Consolidation) Act 1978, s 84*]. An employee must claim a redundancy payment within six months of his dismissal. An employer has a duty to consult with employees and any recognised trade union where redundancies are proposed and may be required to inform the Secretary of State.

Unfair dismissal

An employee who is dismissed with in most cases two years qualifying service may claim for unfair dismissal. It is then for the employer to show that the dismissal was fair and was for one of five potentially fair reasons, namely – capability, conduct, redundancy, to avoid contravention of any statute, or for 'some other substantial reason'. [*Employment Protection (Consolidation) Act 1978, s 57(1)(2)*]. An employer must show that he acted reasonably in all the circumstances in reaching a decision to dismiss and procedural fairness is extremely important in determining whether the dismissal is unfair. It is deemed automatically unfair for an employer to dismiss an employee for belonging or refusing to belong to a trade union (*Trade Union and Labour Relations (Consolidation) Act 1992*) for asserting a statutory right or reasons connected with pregnancy or certain health and safety matters (*Employment Protection (Consolidation) Act 1978 s 57(3)*), when no qualifying service may be necessary. An employee with two years' qualifying service may demand a written statement giving the reasons for his dismissal. [*Employment Protection (Consolidation) Act 1978, s 53*]. The claim must be made to a tribunal within three months of the date of dismissal. If the dismissal is found to be unfair, the tribunal may order re-instatement or re-engagement or, most commonly, compensation.

Maternity rights

A pregnant woman has various statutory maternity rights depending on her length of service, including time off for ante-natal care, the right not to be unfairly dismissed for reasons connected to the pregnancy, maternity pay, a right to return to work and also a right not to be discriminated against on the grounds of her pregnancy. The provisions are complex and should be checked in every case.

Miscellaneous

Other acts which may be of particular relevance to the working conditions of an employee and reflect upon his employment status are the following.

(*a*) The *Shops Act 1950* which regulates hours of work of those people employed in catering premises including public areas of restaurants and hotels.

(*b*) The *Health and Safety at Work etc. Act 1974* which deals with health and safety of employees at work and imposes a legal duty on employers to ensure, so far as reasonably practical, the health, safety and welfare of all employees at work. An employer must provide a written statement of his general policy with respect to the health and safety at work. It also extends to employee liability in that employees are responsible for ensuring not only their own health and safety but also that of their colleagues.

(*c*) The *Office, Shops and Railway Premises Act 1963* which covers employees of restaurants and certain hotels providing for basic working conditions in respect of health and welfare, sanitation and water, seating and work space, employees safety in respect of the premises, the machinery, fire prevention and first aid.

(*d*) European law and European case law is constantly developing and has profound influence on the rights and duties of employees and employers.

(e) *Sunday Trading Act 1994* – Employers with employees working in shop concessions within a hotel (other than those selling refreshments or meals) should also be aware of the provisions of the *Sunday Trading Act 1994*. This provides protection for certain categories of employees, namely those employed as at 26 August 1994 (but not employed only to work on Sundays) and those workers employed under a contract of employment under which they cannot be required to work Sundays. Dismissal of such workers for refusing to work on Sundays will be automatically unfair without the need for two years' qualifying service. Similarly, such workers have the right not to suffer any detriment for refusing to work on Sundays.

Employees can waive this protection by giving written notice to their employer agreeing to work on Sundays. Conversely, employees who may be required under the terms of their contract of work on Sundays (but who are not employed only to work on Sundays) must be given a prescribed form of notice by their employer. Such employees may give their employer a notice stating that they object to Sunday working. After the expiry of three months, such an employer will then have the same protection as those employees detailed above.

Chapter 4

Property and Valuation

Background

4.1   The background of the hotel industry has been considered in an earlier chapter, but the following property aspects shine through in relation to the current market place.

(*a*)   A division between large city/urban centre hotels primarily corporately owned, and smaller provincial hotels and inns typically privately owned.

(*b*)   Much of the existing stock of accommodation is not in first class condition due to indifferent development during the early 1970s as a result of government subsidy, and the attitude to planned maintenance adopted by many hoteliers exacerbated by low profitability over recent years.

(*c*)   Following the recent recession and collapse of the hotel market amidst claims that insolvency practitioners were the largest hotel proprietor, two factors have arisen. First, it is difficult to raise finance for acquisitions in the sector from traditional lending sources, particularly for individual acquisitions, but this will ease in line with recovery. In addition, a level playing field now exists from which a sensible hotel market and hotel property values may arise based primarily upon the trading ability of the business.

Classification of hotels

4.2   According to statistics provided by the British Tourist Authority, there are currently in excess of 42,000 hotels in Great Britain (see 2.2 above).

From an operational viewpoint, however, the hotel property market can conveniently be divided into firstly city or urban centre hotels, and secondly their provincial counterparts. Although some overlap between the two will inevitably result, they tend to have very different characteristics.

City/urban centre hotels

4.3   These can conveniently be divided into the following bands which to an extent follow broadly the star gradings adopted by various organisations,

34

including the Automobile Association, the Royal Automobile Club and the Regional Tourist Boards (see 2.4 above).

(*a*) *Flagship or trophy hotels* – These are luxury five star hotels, which until recently were generally to be found in London (exceptions to this rule included hotels such as Gleneagles). Recently, however, five star hotels have been constructed in city centres outside London, and in some instances refurbished hotels are now attaining five star status. Such an hotel would typically offer uniformed staff, luxurious en-suite bedrooms, spacious public rooms with cocktail facilities available, the highest international standards of cuisine, flower shops and hairdressing salons, cinema facilities, private function rooms and extensive recreational facilities, such as squash courts, swimming pool and games room for children.

(*b*) *Business hotels* – Business hotels traditionally attract three or four star ratings and are found in most major city centre and urban locations, typically offering up to 150 bedrooms. They tend to provide comfortable and spacious en-suite bedrooms depending upon the actual star rating, comfortable public lounges with refreshments available, and some recreational and leisure facilities.

(*c*) *Budget hotels/lodges* – During the 1980s we saw the entry of the budget hotel or lodge based upon a modular low priced design aimed at the lower end of the business market and offering quality en-suite accommodation sold on a value for money basis following the successful French format located often in commercial or industrial areas. Typically having a one or two star category, budget hotels/lodges usually have between 20 and 60 bedrooms, and provide a functional but clean and comfortable bedroom facility, ideally suited for travelling businessmen, with bedrooms usually providing centrally heated accommodation, tea and coffee making facilities, televisions, working surfaces, trouser presses, electric hairdryers and en-suite facilities. Sometimes the hotel's restaurant facilities are found within a nearby restaurant block, which may be under the same ownership as the hotel.

(*d*) *Resort hotels* – During the nineteenth century, the development of railways, and the expansion of tourism that followed, led to the railway companies developing their own hotels. This led to the development of other hotels built to serve seaside towns and country spa towns. It is significant that whilst there are many successful hotels within this sector of the market, the success of resort hotels can be materially influenced by external factors, such as the weather, changing public fashions, tastes and holiday location requirements. Many of these establishments find themselves currently in the unenviable 'Catch 22' downward spiral created by a deteriorating quality of accommodation and insufficient profitability to enable refurbishment. Due to changing holiday patterns, seaside towns today suffer from an over-supply of this type of accommodation, which has been particularly badly hit during the recent recession.

(*e*)   *Guest houses/hostels* – This category includes primarily family run converted residential accommodation and represents a substantial element of the overall market. They are frequently owned and run by individuals and whilst there are examples of good quality and value for money enterprises, the majority are trading out of old-fashioned accommodation and lack the profitability to improve the business and their facilities. This sector of the market also includes many large private hostels, particularly in London.

Provincial hotels

4.4   The provincial hotel, lying outside the city centre and major urban area, again covers a wide range of properties used both for leisure and business purposes.

(*a*)   *Country house hotels* – The country house hotel market currently represents about 1 per cent of the total hotel market, and is aimed at a combination of weekend breaks with tourists and holiday makers, and weekday business custom depending upon the proximity of the hotel to a large population centre or major road/intersection. A country house hotel typically provides between 20 and 70 bedrooms, some having small leisure and health and fitness clubs, and golf facilities. These hotels are typically difficult to market due to location, high operational costs and the elasticity of demand for luxury accommodation, which suffers during recessionary economic conditions. A number of groups have been formed to market the product, the leader being perhaps Relais et Chateaux.

The Royal & Ancient Golf Club of St Andrews report on the need for additional golf courses up to the year 2000 in the UK created, in many farmers' minds, a panacea for their problems associated with dwindling farm incomes. This led to a great number of planning permissions being granted for golf courses and golf hotels. Some were not taken up, and some were, but through poor advice, over optimistic trading forecasts and ill timing or a combination of these, some became insolvent. The golf hotel concept was, however, taken forward corporately by Whitbread under their Country Club Hotels banner, using the slogan 'Country Locations with City Connections' to emphasise their accessibility to motorways.

(*b*)   *Budget motel/lodge* – The value for money, convenient budget lodge was developed along with other roadside facilities in the provinces, much along the lines of the budget lodges (see 4.3 above), under the city/urban centre category. They grew primarily with companies like

Granada, Trust House Forte, Campanile and Accor being located on motorway and other services, main 'A' roads and at intersections.

(*c*)   *Health and fitness hotels* – A number of establishments have been developed and have flourished, particularly during the 1980s, specialising in recuperative confinement and treatment of certain medical disorders including slimming and certain drug-related conditions. A quality operation with clinical referrals can form the basis for a good business, but the market is small and specialised.

Other concepts

4.5   A number of other concepts are currently being examined including:

(*a*)   Serviced accommodation – where extended length bookings are encouraged. The accommodation includes private internal catering facilities.

(*b*)   Hospital or patient care hotels – where patients not requiring day-to-day intensive nursing can be accommodated at a much lower cost per bed space than would be the case in a state or private hospital, usually during the pre-operational or convalescent stage.

(*c*)   Retirement hotels – this concept is now being developed with studio flats, one and two bedroomed apartments being made available on a monthly basis. In-house medical assistance is not provided and the schemes are directed towards the active elderly who might otherwise consider sheltered housing, but prefer and can afford a more luxurious hotel lifestyle.

(*d*)   Hotel and conference centre joint ventures – a number of companies are considering reducing the cost of their existing facilities for corporate training by forming joint ventures with hoteliers.

Property aspects

4.6   Even though a new entrant into the hotel market purchasing an existing hotel will be primarily concerned with the existing business, the capacity for growth and improved profitability, he must never lose sight of the fact that the property is the conduit through which that income flows and any proposal he may have will in one way or another involve, or be dependent upon, the property. For that reason, some basic aspects need to be taken into account.

Location

4.7   Most students of land economics will have been taught at the commencement of their studies that location, being the single unique element of any property, is fundamental to the success and profitability of the enterprise being undertaken from the premises. It is, as a result, the most important factor in determining the value of the property. In relation to hotels, the strengths and weaknesses of the location should be taken into account and the threats posed by road improvement or traffic management schemes, one-way systems, pedestrianisation, bypasses, compulsory purchase orders, and increased competition from either new development or upgrading.

The hotel

4.8   First impressions are equally important whether you intend to stay in an hotel for one night or buy it. It is therefore necessary for an operator or vendor to present the hotel in its very best light. Equally as a purchaser it is necessary to look underneath the marketing veneer to establish whether the structure of the business is sound or not. Whilst an 'olde worlde' environment, or period façade, may exude the right ambience, it is rare to find an old building, even if it has been recently converted to an hotel, which is as efficient to run as a well planned modern hotel. It will lack the ability of the latter to increase income from higher customer convenience, due to easy parking and clean, modern, air conditioned, quieter accommodation. In addition, overheads can be cut by reducing a well planned hotel's staffing ratios and servicing, fuel and maintenance costs. Regular expenditure can be incurred on older buildings to maintain similar qualities of accommodation, but this will impact upon profitability. A number of conversion projects have been undertaken over the last ten years of former mansions, multi-storey factories, warehouses, mills and other institutional properties, and some of these have been more successful than others. Generally, those projects which have been successful have achieved an equilibrium between consumer demand and the type of facilities provided at a realistic price balanced against prudent borrowing criteria. On-site car parking is increasingly important and where this is insufficient, private and public car parking facilities should be examined together with the local authority car parking policy. Consideration should also be given to neighbouring uses in order to identify potential problems, or spin-offs and potential for enlarging the property through site assembly. It is also important to be aware of adjoining uses that may increase insurance premiums, i.e. dangerous neighbouring uses, electrical sub-stations and rivers.

Accommodation and site

4.9   A constrained site will always lead to operational problems and will inhibit the possibility for future extensions and flexibility for alternative uses. The accommodation should be well planned and capable of being improved and in good repair. Fixtures and fittings will need to be documented and assessed between those items to be included in the sale and those to be removed or sold separately. A stocktaker will be appointed to provide a valuation of the consumable stock and glassware on the date of sale.

Tenure/title

4.10   The vast majority of hotels are held on a freehold basis. It is, however, quite common for hoteliers to lease fixtures, fittings and equipment. It is therefore important to clarify precisely which fittings, if any, are leased and what arrangements will be required by the finance company to continue the leasing arrangements or more likely to pay a capital sum to bring the leasing arrangements to an end.

It is worth noting that whilst bankers have historically often accepted simply a fixed first charge over the property, the large number of insolvencies which have occurred over the last few years have proved, in the case of a trading business, that it is imperative for the bank or the bank's appointed receivers to be able to sell the property as a trading entity. Therefore a fixed and floating charge would be required to cover not only the property but also the fixtures, fittings, trade contents and equipment which may otherwise be removed thereby inhibiting a sale as a trading entity.

Solicitors can provide a report on title and particularly with older properties it is surprising how many blemishes are found on the title including boundary inconsistencies and restrictive covenants, including problems with vehicle parking or access. Following the reduction of the main brewers' tied estates after the 1989 Monopolies and Mergers Commission Report, the number of leasehold pubs has risen substantially but there are still very few leasehold hotels. This has created a situation whereby there are now few examples of comparable leases and lease terms which has tended to create a number of leases with onerous terms, often in favour of the landlord, and which can have a particularly adverse effect upon rent reviews and the open market value of the leasehold interest. Problems are usually built in during the drafting of the lease when the parties are unable to agree on an appropriate format for the rent review, and as a result these are often linked into the higher of various alternative bases. Some leasehold hotels, after only a relatively small number of years of the term have expired, are subject to such high rental streams that they erode not only the income which should be enjoyed by the tenant, but also all of the profits. As a result sooner or later the business fails (see 4.30 below).

Problems can also be encountered in relation to alienation, user, repairing covenants, and dilapidations liability. Accordingly, whilst a leasehold hotel may appear to provide a low capital requirement route into the hotel industry, it is an area with potential pitfalls upon which specialist legal and valuation advice is needed.

Rating

4.11   The current rateable value and rates payable figures should be made available in relation to each property and where the hotel includes a pure residential element this is excluded from the assessment and the property is described as a composite. Prior to purchasing an hotel, or undertaking major works, professional advice should be obtained upon whether the current assessment can be reduced or alternatively what effect improvements will have upon the existing assessment. It should be noted that on some marginal businesses, a small reduction in outgoings following a successful appeal, transforms the overall profitability. The new rateable value based on rental values as at 1 April 1993 came into force on 1 April 1995 (see Chapter 8).

Town planning

4.12   It is important to obtain confirmation that the existing buildings have all the necessary consents and that there are no outstanding matters which could have a cost or more onerous implication. It is also wise to obtain a view upon the acceptability of further extensions and indeed the planning authority's view upon any alternative uses that may be more valuable (see 3.10 above).

The local authority are the main source of information regarding other developments which may improve, or worsen, the hotel's trade and they can inform you of their policy towards hotel development. Hotels may be statutorily listed as Grade I, Grade II* or Grade II by the DoE. *Class C1* of the *Town and Country Planning (Use Classes) Order 1987 (SI 1987 No 764)* includes hotels, whilst hostels were removed from this category on 1 April 1994.

Do not be fooled into a warm comfortable belief that because a building is listed it must have historical merit, and therefore must be more attractive and valuable. The truth of the matter is that, at best, everything you want to do to the building will cost you considerably more than it would if it were not listed, and at worst, you would not be able to undertake any of the alterations that you might wish to.

Trading information

4.13   Given that hotels usually change hands in the open market at prices which are based directly on the property's trading potential, it is important that the purchaser and his valuer have a sound knowledge and understanding of the type of business which is carried on at the particular hotel.

In order to arrive at a valuation, the valuer should *inter alia* analyse and review the certified trading accounts of the hotel for the previous three or more years, the current year, and any projections for future years, to form an opinion as to the future fair maintainable trade, and maintainable operating profits, which are likely to be achieved by an efficient operator. It is crucial that, when analysing the previous trading accounts, the valuer discounts any unusual peaks or troughs of a non-recurring nature, e.g. individual items of expenditure such as a major repair to the roof or trading fluctuations caused by external factors such as the Gulf War, which would not be expected to occur either in the current, or future years, and would not, therefore, impact upon the property's fair maintainable trade.

It should also be noted that the trading accounts of a particular property will only show how that property is trading under the existing management. The valuer's expertise is therefore needed to assess the future fair maintainable turnover and profitability, which could be achieved by an efficient operator of the business, and this would reflect the inherent goodwill of the property, i.e. the trading potential which runs with the property by virtue of its location, design, planning permission and licenses. It is crucial, however, that personal goodwill, which has been created in the business by the present owner or management, and which could be transferred to another property should the owner vacate, is excluded from the valuation. Conversely, the valuer should include any additional trading potential which might be realised, if the hotel was in the hands of a more efficient operator (see 4.21 *et seq.* below).

Licences and certificates

4.14   When hotels are sold as fully operational businesses, the ingoing purchaser will, as a rule, expect to renew the various licences and consents, and take over the benefit of existing certificates and permits. These may vary from hotel to hotel, and between different areas of the UK. However, the most commonly found include:

(*a*)   a full Justices' On-Licence, entitling the sale of alcohol for consumption either on or off the premises;

(*b*)   a restaurant licence, which permits the sale of alcohol to persons taking table meals, and as an ancillary to the meal, but those who are not taking table meals are not permitted to consume alcohol;

(*c*)   a residential licence, which permits intoxicating liquor to be sold to residents only, and who may drink without eating. These forms of licence are often granted in respect of premises which provide board and lodging, and small hotels;

(*d*)   a restaurant certificate (formerly known as a supper hour certificate) which enables hotels to serve intoxicating liquor to diners for an hour after the end of ordinary pub licensing hours;

(*e*)   a public entertainments licence, which is required for premises which provide entertainments, including music and dancing;

(*f*)   a special hours certificate, which permits late night functions, but which may be limited to particular times of the day or the week;

(*g*)   an occasional licence, which permits licencees to sell intoxicating liquor either on another part of their premises, or on other premises; and (*h*)   an off-licence, which permits the sale of intoxicating liquor for consumption off the premises.

(See 3.13 *et seq.* above.)

The existence of any or all of these licences is crucial to the trading ability of the hotel, and the loss of any licence is likely to lead to a decline in the fair maintainable trade and value. In view of the importance of the licences and consents to the ongoing business of the hotel, the valuer should, wherever possible, inspect all such documents relating to the property. It is to be recommended that, whilst the valuer should generally assume that an hotel will continue to trade with all existing consents, permits and certificates, he should nevertheless point out that the value could be reduced if the licences were lost or were in jeopardy.

Fire, health and safety

4.15   The purchaser must establish whether a valid Fire Certificate has been granted under the *Fire Precautions Act 1971* and, if necessary, reflect in his bid the cost of any necessary remedial works. The purchaser should also check with the appropriate authority whether any outstanding works need to be undertaken to the property under environmental health and food safety regulations, including the *Food Safety Act 1990* and *Food and Hygiene (Amendment) Regulations 1990 (SI 1990 No 1431).*

Competition

4.16   It is considered by some that local competition is a positive factor in that it ensures that the hotelier keeps on his toes and avoids complacency which can have the effect of eroding his market share. Local competition can also lead to public awareness of hotel facilities in an area. Nonetheless, when undertaking a review of an hotel, it is important that the prospective purchaser quantifies in his business plan the effect of any new competition, and other external factors which can have a dramatic effect on the profitability of an hotel, and hence its value.

Services and systems

4.17   A full engineers report on mains services including water quality, drainage, central heating systems, lifts, and other plant is recommended prior to proceeding with the acquisition of an hotel. The report should not only address the condition of the systems but also the annual running cost, and the cost and timing of repairs and replacements.

Structural survey

4.18   Hoteliers are not noted generally for their care of the fabric of hotel buildings particularly those parts not open to the clientele, neither are they converts to a planned maintenance policy. Indeed, many hoteliers consider themselves to be expert contractors and project managers as well as hoteliers and as a result a structural survey by a building surveyor is often worthwhile. It is recommended practice that a sinking fund is created to meet the costs of future repairs and maintenance.

Alternative uses

4.19   It is relatively rare to find a situation where an up to date profitable hotel will have a higher alternative use value taking into account conversion or demolition costs. However, situations where it might occur include the following:

(*a*)   it is occupying a prime city centre office or retail site;

(*b*)   it is occupying an out of town food store site;

(*c*)   it is needed as part of another development and enjoys a strategic ransom position; or

(*d*)   it has a special purchaser value.

Less profitable hotels may have relatively valuable alternative uses and this should be examined when making an acquisition. Such potential alternative uses for the building or the site, in addition to those set out above, may include residential, flats, nursing homes or other uses which will always be governed by planning, highway issues, statutory and other relevant constraints.

Capital allowances

4.20   The capital allowances inherent within an hotel are a valuable resource. When evaluating an hotel, they should be quantified in terms of the amount available for plant and machinery allowances, which can be a function of purchase price, and in terms of industrial buildings allowances which are a function of historic costs of construction when incurred in the last 25 years. The reason for their importance is not only as a tax advantage to the purchaser or disadvantage to the vendor, but as a component of a funding or financing package. Tax efficient structures such as hotels are often financed using inherent tax breaks to reduce borrowing costs. In any event they are a resource that should never be ignored (see 7.8 below).

Valuation aspects

4.21   At its simplest, a valuation is an independent assessment of the value of an asset. This can encompass a building, a business, an area of land, plant and machinery or work in progress. To a chartered surveyor, there is more than one type of valuation, because the value of an asset depends on the purpose for which it is being valued. In certain circumstances, value means 'the price you could sell it for today on the open market'. In other circumstances value might be 'how much it would cost to replace or reinstate'. These values could be very different. For example, a rundown listed Palladian style country house hotel in the grip of recession may only receive bids of £1 million from prospective purchasers, but its replacement cost could be three times that sum.

For this reason, it is vital to identify which type of valuation is required, and the nature of the interest which is being valued. There has recently been considerable debate in the hotel industry over valuations which have been provided during the last few years. Problems have arisen for the following reasons:

(*a*)   inexperienced valuers;

(*b*)   unqualified reliance upon optimistic projected income streams;

(*c*)   reliance upon 'comparable' evidence derived from an artificial 'frothy' market in the late 1980s, rather than the business's ability to support borrowings;

(*d*)   wrong valuation bases being adopted; or

(*e*)   poor lending decisions.

The issue of the correct approach to hotel valuations came to a head in 1993 when it became known that two firms of valuers had produced valuations many hundreds of millions of pounds apart in respect of the value of a major hotel portfolio.

In March 1994, the Royal Institution of Chartered Surveyors (RICS) issued a new valuation guidance note (VGN13) relating to the capital valuation of hotel, leisure and licensed properties, to compliment the RICS Statements of Asset Valuation Practice and Guidance Notes (the Red Book). It was emphasised that the new guidance notes were not directly concerned with the valuation method, but rather with the practical approach to valuation including the assembly, interpretation and reporting of relevant information.

In December 1993 the British Association of Hotel Accountants (BAHA) produced their own recommended practice for the valuation of hotels and in August 1994, the RICS released their response to the BAHA document. The debate has been wide ranging and one of the main areas of concern has been whether the recommended valuation technique should be the adoption of the discounted cashflow approach, as advocated by BAHA, or the income capitalisation (earnings multiple) approach advocated by the RICS.

The valuation of hotels should be undertaken only by those chartered surveyors who are fully conversant with the recognised valuation methods and state of market conditions, to enable them to provide full, proper and accurate advice, in accordance with the Guidance Notes.

The New Red Book

4.22   Following concern expressed at a number of levels about commercial property valuations, the RICS set up a working party chaired by Michael Mallinson to consider the overall position and they reported in March 1994. Criticisms ranged from dissatisfaction with valuation bases and methodologies and how they are used, to deficiencies in the way valuers present and explain their work. The working party's recommendations sought to assist in attaining the goals of greater credibility, reliability and clarity in the provision of commercial property valuations.

Immediately prior to the publication of this book, the RICS published the new Appraisal and Valuation Manual (known as the New Red Book) which adopted many of the Mallinson report recommendations. It is the most comprehensive code of valuation practice yet devised anywhere in the world and comes into force on 1 January 1996. For the sake of convenience and increased clarity, the new manual is an amalgam of the existing Red and White Books containing Statements of Asset Valuation Practice and Guidance Notes. The practice statements are mandatory for all hotel valuations with limited exceptions, the most important of which are in respect of reports prepared for marketing purposes.

In terms of valuation bases, definition and guidance, the new manual generally follows the same basic rationale for the preparation of hotel valuations where they are prepared for accounts purposes, loan security or otherwise. However, there are new rules for the way in which valuers are engaged for different types of valuation and the scope and content of their reports.

As before, hotels which are trading come within the general category of land and buildings fully equipped as an operational entity and valued having regard to trading potential. The appropriate basis of valuation is now Open Market Value (OMV) or Existing Use Value (EUV), which basically follows the previous definition of open market value for the existing use as described below. There is an added assumption that the hypothetical parties to the transaction had acted knowledgeably, prudently and without compulsion. The New Red Book, whilst generally following the previous guidance contained within VGN 13, acknowledges that different valuation methods may be appropriate including the profits method, discounted cashflow, analysis of comparable transactions or a combination of these. In any event, the valuation method should reflect the approach generally used by the market.

There is further guidance for the valuer when providing loan security valuation reports on the opinion which should be given as to the sustainability of the hotel business and the need to advise with regard to possible future fluctuations in trade affecting the hotel's status as a security in the longer term.

It is expected that the new manual will substantially improve the valuer's ability to understand and service clients' requirements for hotel valuation, whilst at the same time raising standards of competence, valuation consistency, reliability and to a degree, the integrity of the valuation product.

Why may valuations be required?

4.23   Hotel valuations may be needed for many purposes and at different times. These purposes include:

(*a*)   acquisition;

(*b*)   sale;

(*c*)   statutory purposes, including compulsory purchase or taxation;

(*d*)   accounts/balance sheet purposes;

(*e*)   loan security;

(*f*)   internal company matters;

(*g*)   joint venture;

(*h*)   investigation by accountants/insolvency practitioners;

(*i*)   rating; and

(*j*)   litigation.

It is crucial that the purpose of the valuation is clarified and agreed in writing between the client and the valuer at the outset of the valuation instruction, in order to avoid any misinterpretation of the basis of valuation to be undertaken.

Types of valuation

4.24   Having established the purpose of the valuation to be undertaken, it is then necessary to identify and agree the appropriate type, or basis of valuation to be undertaken.

These are defined under the Red Book prepared by the RICS, and these may be summarised as follows.

Open market value for the existing use

This basis of valuation is appropriate for properties which are designed or adapted for particular uses, and which invariably change hands in the open market at prices based directly on trading potential for a strictly limited use, including hotels. The operational entity includes, beside the land and building, items such as fixtures, furniture, goodwill and stock at valuation. The valuation reflects the valuer's opinion as to the best price at which the interest in the property might reasonably be expected to have been completed unconditionally for cash consideration at the date of the valuation, assuming that the property will continue to be owner-occupied for the existing use and that the market remains constant. It should reflect any special adaptations, or particular suitability of the premises for the existing use, but excludes any element of value attributable to an alternative use. Similarly, the valuation should include any value attributable to any possibilities of extensions or further buildings on undeveloped land, or redevelopment of existing buildings (all for the existing use), provided that such construction can be undertaken without major interruption to the continuing business. A fundamental assumption is that prior to the date of valuation, there had been a reasonable period (having regard to the nature of the property and the state of the market) for the proper marketing of the interest for the agreement of price and terms, and for the completion of the sale. It is also important that in the valuation, no account is taken of any additional bid by a purchaser with a special interest, and that the vendor is a willing seller. In the case of an hotel, it would be appropriate in a valuation, for the valuer to use words such as 'open market value for the existing use as a fully operational hotel'.

Forced sale value

It is a popular misconception in the hotel industry that 'forced sale value' is an accepted valuation basis. The Red Book states that in the case of properties valued by reference to their trading potential, including hotels, the expression 'forced sale value' is not valid and is not to be used under any circumstances. It is recognised, however, that there is a clear need for a valuation basis upon which lenders can rely in the event of default, i.e. when, as a result of the owners' failure to pay interest and/or capital, the property is to be placed on the market at the insistence of the lender.

The appropriate valuation basis, in this case, is Value in the Event of Default, which has now, in effect replaced the previous expression of forced sale value.

A valuation in the event of default applies to properties which are fully equipped as an operational entity, being valued having regard to trading potential, i.e. including hotels. This valuation basis reflects open market value, but assumes:

(*a*)   the vendor has imposed an undue time constraint for securing completion of the disposal;

(*b*)   the accounts, or records of trade, would not be available to, or relied upon by a prospective purchaser; and

(*c*)   the business is open for trade.

The valuer must agree with his client the period of the assumed undue time constraint to be adopted in the valuation. He should point out to the lender that the reported value could be lower if a number of scenarios were to occur, including:

(i)   the business were to be closed;

(ii)   the inventory were removed;

(iii) the justices or other licences and/or certificates were lost or are in jeopardy; or

(iv)   the property were to be vandalised.

Bricks and Mortar Valuation

In the same way that requests for forced sale valuations are made, a valuer on occasions may also be asked for a 'Bricks and Mortar' valuation, supposedly representing the open market value of the land and buildings element of the trading entity.

Whilst an apportionment can be made by isolating from the total value of the trading entity those elements relating only to the land and buildings, this would involve excluding the elements related to the tenants' furniture, fixtures and fittings, statutory consents, licences and permits, and goodwill attaching to the property. Although this is arguably possible as a hypothetical exercise, it is not a recognised valuation basis and for this reason, the valuer may be asked to refer to the open market value for an alternative use, with vacant possession.

Alternative use value

In certain circumstances changes in fashion or demand for hotels may make it necessary to have regard to the alternative use value of a property. This basis of valuation effectively provides the lender with a valuation backstop, should for any reason the hotel business fail, and the property have to be sold for its best alternative use. The alternative use value must relate to definite information regarding statutory consents, change of use and, if this information is not available, appropriate assumptions should be agreed with the client and stated in the valuation certificate.

Estimated Realisation Price

All of the valuation bases defined above assume that the value is correct at the date of valuation and that the property would have been marketed during an appropriate period leading up to the date of the valuation. However, with effect from March 1994, under VGN 12, following discussion with the banking industry, the RICS have introduced an additional basis of valuation, known as Estimated Realisation Price. The fundamental difference, with this basis, is that the valuer shall give his opinion of the amount of cash consideration which he believes could reasonably be expected to be obtained for the interest in the property on completion of an unconditional sale on an assumed date, and following an appropriate period of marketing. This could be between three and twelve months into the future, or shorter or longer if required. It may be appreciated that the difference between the two will become more marked in a rising or falling market.

Estimated Restricted Realisation Price

This reflects the basis of Estimated Realisation Price above, but the period available to achieve a sale is assumed to be any such lesser period as the lender may specify.

Reinstatement Cost Assessment

This should not be confused with other valuations, as it reflects the likely cost of reinstating all the buildings, normally for insurance purposes. It does not reflect the price which may be achieved for the property on the open market, either at the date of the valuation or at an assumed date in the future.

Investment Valuation

Investment Valuations, which will usually be subject to a lease, are to be carried out in accordance with Open Market Value.

Open market rental value

Open market rental value is the rental level that a property would have achieved had it been offered to let in the market and the letting completed at the valuation date. The rent would reflect all aspects of the property including the terms of the lease, which usually receives special comment in the valuation. Negotiations between landlords and tenants frequently call for an assessment of open market rental value.

Valuation principles and methods

4.25   The valuation method to be adopted by the valuer should reflect the approach generally used by the market for the particular type of property under consideration. Accordingly, different methods, including the profits method (or income capitalisation approach), analysis of comparable transactions, the discounted cashflow method, or indeed, a combination of all of these, may be appropriate for different types and sizes of hotel. Ultimately, the basis or bases of valuation used must reflect the approach which is used within that particular sector of the hotel market place.

As hotels are generally valued by reference to their actual trading performance and/or trading potential, hotels are valued on the basis of open market value for the existing use, as a fully equipped operational entity. The resulting valuation of the operation includes:

(*a*)   the land and buildings;

(*b*)   trade, contents, fixtures, fittings, furniture, furnishings and equipment;

(*c*)   inherent goodwill, which reflects the trading potential which runs with the property but excludes personal goodwill which reflects any turnover or profit which is attributable solely to the personal skill, expertise and reputation of the owner and which may be transferable to another property; and

(*d*)   an assumed ability to renew existing licences, consents, certificates and permits.

It is important to note that consumable stocks should be excluded from the valuation.

Profits method/income capitalisation approach

4.26   The traditional method of valuation for hotels is the profits method, or income capitalisation approach. The valuer, as a rule, should obtain at least three years' certified trading accounts, and future projections. From his experience in the hotel market, he should be able to form an opinion as to the hotel's fair maintainable trade.

The hotels' accounts usually indicate receipts, and costs, net of VAT. The receipts, or turnover, are typically divided between the three principal areas of trade, namely accommodation, food, and wet sales. Its gross profit levels are usually arrived at by deducting the costs of food and wet sales from the turnover levels. To arrive at its net profit levels, it is necessary to deduct from the gross profit, all the expenses relating to the hotel, including operational expenses, financial expenses, and expenses relating to the property. An example of a typical provincial hotel's trading accounts, and a valuation on this basis, is set out overleaf.

The resultant valuation figure provides the valuation of the hotel, freehold, including non-personal goodwill and trade contents. The valuation excludes wet and dry stock and any items which may be of a personal nature, and owned by the hotelier.

Profits method/income capitalisation approach – valuation example

Sales	£	£
Accommodation		1,000,000
Food		600,000
Liquor/Wet Sales		400,000
Sundries		75,000
TOTAL SALES		2,075,00
Less Purchases and Cost of Sales		
Food	200,000	
Drink	150,000	350,000
Gross Profit		1,725,000
Less Working Expenses		
Wages and Staff Costs	650,000	
Insurance	15,000	
Lighting and heating	40,000	
Repairs, renewals and maintenance	50,000	
Rates	65,000	
Laundry	5,000	
Printing and stationery	15,000	
Telephone and postage	10,000	
Staff training	25,000	
Accountancy fees	15,000	
Legal fees	5,000	
Bank charges	5,000	
Depreciation	75,000	
Bank interest	250,000	1,225,000
Net Profit		500,000

Add back any extraodinary items of expenditure, to arrive at fair maintainable adjusted net profit, before director's fees, bank interest, depreciation and tax.

Depreciation	75,000	
Bank interest	250,000	325,000
Adjusted Net Profit		825,000
Years purchase in perpetuity @ 14%		7.14
Open market value for the existing use as a fully operational hotel		5,890,500
	say	5,900,000

When considering a hotel's trading accounts, it is important to build up a picture of the hotel's fair maintainable trade, by obtaining at least the previous three years' trading accounts. Purchasers should, however, beware of hotels where the hotel's sales are derived from one particular client, e.g. a local industrialist, particularly if there is no ready supply of trade from other clients.

In such cases, a purchasing hotelier would expect to reflect a higher yield in his valuation, when considering his bid.

It will also be helpful for the purchaser and his valuer to consider whether the hotel lends itself to expansion, in which case economies of scale may be derived. The cost of servicing an hotel of, for example, 40 bedrooms, is unlikely to be much greater than the cost of servicing a hotel of half that size and, by increasing the letting capacity of the hotel, it may be possible to generate extra turnover, a high proportion of which can be taken as profit. Before embarking upon such a scheme, however, it is important to ensure that the hotel's public facilities, including the bar and restaurant, are able to accommodate the extra trade. Ultimately, the yield to be used in hotel valuations will vary, according to the location of the hotel, the likely demand in the market place, the type of prospective purchaser that would exist and the attractiveness or otherwise of the fair maintainable turnover and profit levels. The valuer will have regard to market evidence of transactions.

Comparable evidence

4.27   To a large extent all valuations rely, to varying degrees, upon comparison with other properties or property transactions. This can involve, in its most unrefined sense, a direct comparison on a letting bedroom basis, down to more sophisticated comparisons of multipliers. A value per bedroom analysis is often hopelessly unreliable and should not be adopted in isolation as a valuation approach.

The discounted cashflow method

4.28   An alternative method of valuation is to value hotels on the basis of potential future earnings growth, rather than recent property transactions. This method uses projected cashflows, and discounted cashflow techniques.

It involves studying management accounts, and profit and loss statements, and by having regard to market conditions, the valuer will usually prepare a ten-year forecast of cashflows. An appropriate discount rate is used to bring the projected cashflows back to present day values. The discount rate will vary between hotels, and the particular characteristics of each hotel being valued will determine *inter alia* the level of risk.

The advantage of this method is that it enables the valuer to consider the possible trading performance of an hotel over the next ten years, and it invites the valuer to build in to the trading forecast any major items of income or expenditure. For example, a new letting bedroom extension which would increase turnover, a rent review, or a major item of repair, which would decrease profitability can be accurately reflected. By taking these and other factors into account, the valuer can arrive at an estimate of the amount which the hotel will actually earn.

It is argued that by adopting the discounted cashflow method of valuation only, in times of exceptionally high demand for hotels, such as the mid-1980s, the resultant valuation could be artificially low. Conversely, in times of recession, such as the early 1990s, when demand for hotels reduced substantially, the resultant valuation could be artificially high.

An example of a simplified discounted cashflow approach is set out below. The example assumes that in the third year, a 50 bedroom extension will be constructed, thereby increasing the capacity of the hotel from 100 bedrooms to 150 bedrooms. The average room rate has been assumed to increase from £60 (year 1), to £95 (year 10), and the occupancy rate is assumed to increase from 50 per cent (year 1) to 75 per cent (year 10). An assumed net profit level, or net cashflow, has been adopted at 35 per cent of turnover received.

Obviously the valuer must use his judgement to form an opinion upon whether the above room and occupancy rates will in fact continue to rise, or be subject to a periodic downturn. Similarly, the valuer should recognise the uncertainty associated with projections of real world events and revenues or costs that flow from those events over a ten-year period. It may be that some valuers will therefore advocate a shorter period, although this may cause problems when considering a new hotel development. Additionally, the valuer should decide upon the appropriate cashflow model to be used in each instance.

The example assumes a sale of the hotel at the end of the period, i.e. at the beginning of year 11 whereby the residual value of the hotel at that time is arrived at by capitalising the net income received by an appropriate capitalisation rate, in this example 13 per cent.

The projected cashflow here, for years 1–10 (inclusive) is discounted by multiplying the net income, or cashflow, by the present value of £1, at the appropriate rate. The total value of the hotel, on this basis, amounts to £11,000,000 after the deduction of the estimated cost of the extension.

It is important to note that the valuation of hotels, whether upon the profits method/income capitalisation approach, or the discounted cashflow method, specifically has regard to the present trade, and the future trading potential of the hotel. As such, the valuation of the hotel on either of these bases will effectively be a valuation of the business and, therefore, adjustments need to be made for any goodwill which would not run with the property, in the hands of another operator. It is crucial when analysing audited or approved management accounts, that any element of turnover which can be ascribed to the goodwill specific to the present operators only, and which would not necessarily be available to the hypothetical purchaser in the open market, is ignored. There are many ways of making suitable adjustments, from a valuation viewpoint, to arrive at the fair maintainable trade.

Discounted cashflow valuation example

	Year 1	Year 2	Year 3	Year 4	Year 5	Year 6	Year 7	Year 8	Year 9	Year 10	Sale 1 Jan Year 11
Bedrooms	100	100	150	150	150	150	150	150	150	150	–
Average Room Rate	£60	£65	£65	£65	£70	£75	£80	£85	£90	£95	–
Occupancy Rate	50%	55%	55%	55%	55%	60%	60%	65%	70%	75%	–
Bedroom Turnover	1,095,000	1,304,875	1,957,312	1,957,312	2,107,875	2,463,750	2,628,000	3,024,937	3,449,250	3,900,937	–
Total Turnover	2,190,000	2,609,750	3,914,624	3,914,624	4,215,750	4,927,500	5,256,000	6,049,874	6,898,500	7,801,874	–
Net income/cashflow taken @ 35% of total turnover after deductions of outgoings	766,500	913,412	1,370,118	1,370,118	1,475,512	1,724,625	1,839,600	2,117,455	2,414,475	2,730,655	–
Cost of Extension	–	–	(2,000,000)	–	–	–	–	–	–	–	–
Projected cashflow	766,500	913,412	-(629,882)	1,370,118	1,475,512	1,724,625	1,839,600	2,117,455	2,414,475	2,730,655	21,005,038
Present value of £1 @ 15%	0.8696	0.7561	0.6575	0.5718	0.4972	0.4323	0.3759	0.3269	0.2843	0.2472	0.2472
DCF/NPV	666,548	690,630	-(414,147)	783,433	733,624	745,555	691,505	692,196	686,435	675,017	5,192,445

Present Value on discounted cash flow basis: 1143241

(Sum of NPV) say £11,000,000

NB: Parry's Valuation and Conversion Tables used. £2,000,000 cost of extension assumes actal cost in Year 3, and not estimated present day cost.

Merits of alternative valuation approach

	Advantages	Disadvantages
Income capitalisation/profits method approach	Traditional and simple valuation method. Gives greater weight to an hotel's achieved performance. Reflects market volatility.	Requires skill of valuers to accurately reflect market conditions and evidence.
Discounted cashflow method	Reflects future income and outgoings. Smooths out volatility of the hotel property market. Useful method of valuation when an hotel is about to be constructed or extended.	Does not reflect extreme market fluctuations. Liable to calculate worth, not value. Value in the event of default or estimated restricted realisation price may prove difficult.

4.29   It is recommended that a number of valuation bases are adopted as cross reference checks upon each other.

Leasehold hotels

4.30   To an hotelier, the attraction of purchasing a leasehold hotel is that it provides the purchaser with a relatively inexpensive opportunity to enter the hotel market, particularly when compared with the prices which are required for freehold hotels. A relatively low capital outlay can secure a business with a high turnover and profit level (see 4.10 above).

The valuation of leasehold hotels generally follows the same principles as the valuation of freehold hotels, being comprised as follows:

(*a*)   value of the land and buildings, being represented by capitalised profit rent;

(*b*)   value of goodwill; and

(*c*)   value of trade fixtures and fittings.

Stock, however, is taken separately at valuation.

When considering the value of the land and buildings element, the valuation will be determined by the level of profit rent, and length of time before the next rent review and the end of the lease. The profit rent may be defined as being the difference between the rental value of the hotel on the open market, and the rent which is payable under the lease. It is crucial that, before entering into a lease, an hotelier receives professional advice generally, but particularly as to the impact of each rent review upon the hotel's business. Hoteliers should also beware of the possibility of the landlord reoccupying the property at the end of the lease term. It is not inconceivable that the landlord, whether he be an individual or a brewery company, may seek to capitalise on the tenant's hard work by repossessing the property at the end of the lease. Ultimately, this will depend upon the nature of the landlord concerned.

Where hotels are held on long leases, for example 99 or 125 years, at a peppercorn rent, or a nominal ground rent, then provided that the lease terms do not contain any unusually onerous conditions, the property can effectively be valued as freehold. However, in more conventional situations, where the profits method or income capital approach is to be adopted, with leases of 20 to 25 years' duration, an adjusted net profit should be calculated after the deduction of the appropriate rental outgoing, and an appropriate yield adopted. Purchasers should beware of leasehold hotels with short unexpired terms of less than 10 years because, if a substantial dilapidations liability attaches to the property, the resultant value may be nil, or even a negative value may exist.

As a general comment, it was evident during the frothy market conditions of the mid-1980s, when there was substantial demand for freehold hotels, leasehold hotels generally commanded premium values, as overall demand exceeded supply throughout the hotel market. The early years of the 1990s have witnessed, however, a collapse in demand for hotels by prospective purchasers and where demand has existed, this has primarily been for the more attractive freehold hotels. As a result, the value of many leasehold hotels has declined substantially, with some becoming unsaleable and being unable to command any element of value on the open market.

Having arrived at the hotel's net profit, items which are known as extraordinary items of expenditure should be added back in to the net profit level, in order to arrive at an adjusted net profit, which is then capitalised at the appropriate multiplier. Such items include non-recurring items of expenditure, for example the cost of a one-off item of repair which is incurred in one year, but not again. Other items to be added back include bank interest charges, depreciation, directors' fees and pensions, together with any items which are peculiar to the actual business and would not be incurred by another operator.

The resultant figure represents the adjusted net profit level, before bank interest, depreciation, and tax.

An example of a valuation of a leasehold hotel, having an unexpired term of 30 years, but being subject to a rent review to full market rental value in four years' time, is provided below:

Leasehold hotel valuation example

(i) *Value of profit rent*

Fair rental value	75,000		
Less rent paid under lease	30,000		
Profit rent	45,000		
YP (until next rent review) 4 years @ 10%, and 3% allowing for tax on sinking fund at rate of 40 pence in the £	2.0065		90,292
			say 90,000

(ii) *Value of goodwill*

Net Profit Level	175,000		
Deduct Profit rent	45,000		
	130,000		
Less interest on: Capital, stock, fixtures and fittings, and cash totalling say £200,000 @ 10%	20,000		
	110,000		
YP	2.5		275,000

(iii) *Value of fixtures and fittings*

Tenants fixtures and fittings		say 150,000
		515,000
Less cost of dilapidations		15,000
Capital value of leasehold interest		£500,000

Hotel acquisition – property checklist

4.31   Generally the purchaser of properties such as residential, industrial, warehouse, office, retail etc. prior to purchase, is faced with satisfying himself or herself that the property, i.e. the land and buildings, are suitable and satisfactory. With an hotel, however, a purchaser needs to have checked, and be assured that not only is the property, i.e. the land and buildings, of suitably sound construction, but also because the purchaser is purchasing a business, all factors relating to the business, and the ability of the business to continue to trade to the purchaser's requirements at the property, needs to have been verified before completion of the purchase takes place.

When a vendor and purchaser agree the terms for the sale of an hotel, and the vendor's and purchaser's respective solicitors are instructed to prepare the contract for sale or lease, the purchaser should have already inspected the property, determined the tenure and, if the property is leasehold, the lease terms, inspected the owner's previous trading accounts and have decided how he will continue and develop the trade.

In a particularly buoyant market, where a number of purchasers are keenly chasing a property, there may be a limited timescale for a purchaser to carry out all necessary investigations into the property and business. Being afraid of possibly losing the opportunity to purchase, a purchaser could submit an offer for an hotel and have it accepted with the usual enquiries being left incomplete, prior to solicitors being instructed. Obviously, such a bold approach is not to be generally recommended. Following the instruction of solicitors, a purchaser must then complete all the necessary enquiries prior to exchange of contract. There is a risk that if such enquiries reveal hidden defects to the property and/or the business, the purchaser may then wish to withdraw and thereby incur abortive legal and other professional costs together with the wrath of the vendor! The nature and state of the hotel market is likely to ultimately determine the time available within which a purchaser has to research and make all necessary and relevant enquiries.

In the ideal world, in conjunction with his professional advisers, particularly his surveyors and accountant, a purchaser would verify all necessary enquiries relating to the purchase before a price is agreed and solicitors are instructed to prepare the sale contract between the vendor and purchaser. If sufficient time is not allowed for all enquiries to have been made before instructing solicitors and agreeing the terms of the sale, it is crucial that these enquiries are made and verified before the exchange of contracts.

The checklist below divides recommended enquiries between the property and the business. The list can not be treated as being exhaustive because of the varying nature of hotels.

The property

4.32

● *Is the property freehold or leasehold?*

Irrespective of the basis of tenure, a land registry plan should be obtained to identify the extent of the property to be purchased or leased and any other relevant factors on the extent of the property and its boundaries, such as rights of way which the property may have, or be subject to, any third party land which may be affected and other factors.

● *Accommodation*

Obviously it is essential that a purchaser is fully aware of the total accommodation comprised within a property to be bought or leased. The vendor's agents' sale particulars should usually provide a schedule of accommodation, but this must have been verified by the purchaser. Preferably the purchaser will be provided with scale floor plans of all of the accommodation, which can then be easily checked by a physical inspection, including room size which can be used to verify the capacity of the hotel.

● *Site area*

The Title Deeds will, as a rule, indicate the physical extent of the property to be bought or leased. However, depending upon the age of the property, it may be difficult to reconcile the precise extent of the boundaries, particularly if the plans are old or the hotel forms part of a large country estate and the plan has been reduced. It is recommended that an Ordnance Survey extract is provided to the purchaser which clearly identifies the extent of the property and its boundaries, together with other relevant factors such as rights of way and access.

● *Services*

The nature and extent of the services to the property can easily be overlooked unless the correct checks are made by a purchaser. The services provided to a property are of such fundamental importance to the operation of the hotel that it is recommended that prior to exchange of contracts, a purchaser instructs a specialist surveyor or engineer to advise upon services. These investigations should include whether the property is connected to mains water, mains drainage, or whether it is connected to a cesspit or septic tank and if so the capacity, cost and frequency of emptying. Investigations should be made to ascertain the capacity of electricity supplied to the property, and whether gas is connected or available close by. The heating system of an hotel is potentially a major source of expenditure and the heating system and source of fuel must be verified.

● *Rating*

The rateable value of the hotel and rates paid must be verified. It should also be borne in mind that the rateable value and occupier's rates liability will be subject to reassessment if improvements or additions are made to the property. Investigations should also be made as to occupier's liability and Council Tax assessments so that the full level of outgoings can be determined.

● *Tenure*

The tenure of the property is of crucial importance and requires formal legal advice. The purchaser's solicitor will advise on the legal extent of the land and buildings, and all matters relating to the property in the Title Deeds, such as covenants, easements, restrictions, liabilities and other matters.

If a prospective tenant is looking to enter into a new lease or take an assignment of an existing lease, the retained solicitors will advise upon all relevant lease terms, including the need for personal guarantees or sureties, mortgages, the existing rent, frequency and basis of rent reviews, the tenants' covenants, including, *inter alia,* repairs, insurance, user, assignment, subletting, keep open/trading obligations, options to break the lease in either the landlord's and/or the tenant's favour, options to purchase the landlord's interest and all other relevant areas of the lease. The surveyor will usually be asked to also advise on lease terms. This is potentially a legal minefield and represents a crucial element of the ingoing purchasers or tenants retained solicitors investigations.

● *Brewery tie*

The purchaser's solicitors must also report upon whether the property is subject to a brewery tie or similar agreement, and if so, the duration and terms of the tie.

● *Fixtures and fittings*

The nature and extent of the fixtures and fittings to be included in the purchase of the hotel must be agreed between the vendor and purchaser and verified between the vendor's and purchaser's representatives as being attached to or within the property. An inventory will be prepared for agreement between the parties, usually by the vendor's surveyors. Certain furniture, fixtures and effects, which may have been seen at the date of the purchaser's visit may actually be the vendor's personal belongings and therefore will be removed from the property prior to sale. The inventory should also refer to all items which are included in the sale, but are on lease, or hire agreements. Again, the purchaser's solicitors will need to obtain confirmation of the terms of such agreements.

As a rule, on the date of completion, the stock take of the food, liquor and consumable items will be prepared for agreement between the vendor and purchaser and the purchaser will usually purchase such items at valuation.

Whilst the extent of fixtures and fittings, contents and stock must be verified by the purchaser's legal representative at completion, it is to be recommended that the purchaser verifies as much of this information as possible prior to instructing solicitors in order to avoid any potential misunderstandings and disappointments at a later stage.

- *Structural survey*

  It is important that before a purchaser exchanges contracts with the vendor, a full structural survey is undertaken by a suitably qualified specialist surveyor to satisfy the purchaser that the property is structurally sound. Structural surveys can be expensive, depending upon the size, form of construction and complexity of the hotel. Nevertheless the cost of a structural survey is one of the most crucial items of expenditure a purchaser will incur when buying an hotel. If the structural survey reveals serious structural defects, the research undertaken will allow the purchaser to either negotiate a suitable adjustment to the price with the vendor, or withdraw and search for an hotel elsewhere. Advice should be obtained on whether the property is liable to matters including subsidence and flooding.

- *Town planning*

  A purchaser should obtain professional advice from a solicitor or a surveyor on town planning matters affecting the property. These will include, *inter alia*, whether there are any local authority redevelopment or road widening proposals which impact upon the property, whether the property is listed, in a conservation area, the planning applications which have been submitted in respect of the property and whether they have been granted, refused, withdrawn or taken to planning appeal. Conditions attached to planning consents require detailed study.

  It is important that a purchaser receives professional advice on whether any previous planning consents may have lapsed, and also whether a purchaser's intentions for the future conversion, improvement, or redevelopment of the property would obtain planning consent. Purchasers of listed buildings should beware because whilst the concept of owning an 'olde worlde' historic and atmospheric hotel may appeal, problems can be encountered at the planning stage when planning and listed building consents need to be obtained for any conversion, adaptation or extension of the property. Listed building consent can be required for alterations to the exterior and interior of the property. Whilst such enquiries are usually not made, a purchaser may wish to obtain advice, or a view, as to the potential alternative uses to which the hotel could be put, should, for any unforeseen reason, the property have to be disposed of for an alternative use. Such enquiries may be made as part of the valuation exercise for bank loan purposes at the time of purchase.

● *Environmental health*

It is essential that the purchaser's solicitor checks the position of the Environmental Health Regulations (which have become increasingly stringent). The necessary enquiries should be made to the Environmental Health Officer at the local authority). This will include whether the Environmental Health Officer has made a recent inspection and issued a letter identifying work to be undertaken.

● *Licences*

The purchaser's solicitor must, prior to exchange of contracts, check the various types of licence which exist, the conditions and restrictions, and oversee the renewal of the licences and certificates to the ingoing purchaser during the transaction.

● *Fire Certificate*

Before purchasing the hotel, the purchaser's representatives must obtain confirmation that a Fire Certificate has been issued under the *Fire Precautions Act 1971* and any relevant amendments or bye-laws. Particular care should be taken to ensure that any recent alterations have been undertaken to the hotel and whether the Fire Officer's written approval has been obtained to any such alterations.

● *Competition*

A purchaser should obtain, or instruct his professional surveyors to obtain, a summary of the competing facilities around the hotel so the ingoing purchaser is clear about the competition. It is advisable that checks are also made with the local planning authority on planning applications which may have been submitted and planning consents which may have been granted in the vicinity which could impact upon the business.

The business

4.33   Having dealt with the checks which a purchaser or his professional advisers should make in relation to the property, detailed investigations must be undertaken in relation to the business. Experienced hoteliers may feel comfortable with analysing the performance of the hotel themselves; but those with less experience may wish to obtain professional advice.

A recommended checklist of matters relating to the business will include the following. Again, this list should not be treated as being exhaustive, but rather a general guide.

●   *Capacity of the hotel*

This should have been ascertained as part of the property enquiries referred to above, including the capacity of the existing bars, restaurants, sleeping capacity, conference facilities, health and fitness accommodation, and other relevant areas of the property.

●   *Customer profile*

The purchaser will need to ascertain the source of the hotel's principal custom, the split between business and tourist related income, recent fluctuations in the popularity of the hotel, and whether the hotel offers potential for increasing trade from the existing, or future potential customers.

●   *The staff*

The purchaser must be clear about the staffing details, including the number of staff employed, their grading, the conditions of employment, wage costs, terms of employment, whether the staff are provided with living accommodation on the premises or proximity to a pool of labour, the frequency of staff turnover and whether the vendor has informed the staff that he intends to dispose of the property. Traditionally, staff can be wary of a change of ownership and they can feel that their jobs may be put in jeopardy due to a possible change in the direction and branding of the hotel, changes in working habits, changes to living accommodation provided, and other factors. It is usually the decision of the vendor to inform the staff of the sale of the hotel. However, it is usually preferable for the vendor and purchaser to meet with the staff at a suitably early stage, e.g. following exchange of contracts, as opposed to imminently before completion, to avoid rumours spreading and hopefully reassure the staff of the purchaser's intentions.

●   *The accounts*

A purchaser should obtain, as a minimum, the previous three years' certified trading accounts relating to the hotel, net of VAT.

It is important to ascertain whether the turnover of the hotel has risen consistently during the three years prior to purchase, declined, or remained stable. Care should be taken where an hotel is effectively operating at near full capacity, as in such cases it may only be possible to increase turnover by price increases – which may be resisted in the market place – or by physically increasing the capacity of the property, e.g. by building an extension. The vendor's trading accounts are likely to reflect the operation of the property to that particular party. The purchaser, therefore, by making the appropriate adjustments to the accounts, needs to arrive at the adjusted net profit level, before owner's salary, bank interest, tax and depreciation. Expert advice should be obtained to ensure that one-off items of expenditure (e.g. a new roof) are not reflected in the year-to-year accounts, and that suitable adjustments are made to reflect items of expenditure which are personal to the existing owner/vendor, e.g. the owner's salary, bank loan interest, tax and depreciation. This is a complex and crucial area of the operation of the business upon which the purchaser should receive specialist professional advice.

Summary

4.34   Historically, there have been a number of different methods of valuing hotels, and there is an ongoing debate about the relative merits of each of these, and the methods of valuation to be adopted in the future. This debate is set to continue in terms of the overall hotel market place. The recession which was evident in the early 1990s has left the industry in a fairly battle weary condition. Confidence was eroded within the hotel industry, and particularly within many financial institutions who had hitherto assisted in funding programmes and lending schemes. However, with growing economic confidence currently returning, the hotel industry is likely to flourish with pre-recession room rates possibly starting to appear with a move away from heavy price discounting and as a result new development and refurbishment of existing buildings are likely to be undertaken as the market improves, underpinned by sensible property values.

In terms of new development, much of the expansion is likely to take place within the budget lodge and business classes of hotel.

Chapter 5

The Audit of Hotels

Introduction

5.1   The majority of hotels in the UK are owned by limited liability companies. Until recently all such active UK companies were required by law to draw up financial statements in accordance with the requirements of the *Companies Act 1985* and for these to be reported upon by a qualified auditor. In November 1993 it was announced by the UK Government that from a date to be specified (later confirmed as 11 August 1994), companies with a turnover of less than £90,000 would no longer require an audit. In addition, companies with turnovers between £90,000 and £350,000 can elect to have an independent accountant's report on whether the company's accounts reflect its books and records, rather than a statutory audit. The requirements, current at the date of writing, with respect to these exemptions and the independent accounts report are dealt with later (see 5.13 below).

A statutory audit in the UK is an examination of the financial statements of an enterprise by an auditor. For companies registered under the *Companies Acts* this has to be performed by a registered auditor. The auditor is required to express an opinion as to whether the financial statements have been properly prepared to show a true and fair view of the state of affairs of the company at the balance sheet date, of its results for the period then ended, whether they comply with accounting standards, financial reporting standards and, where applicable, with company law.

The audit report

5.2   When reporting under the *Companies Act*, auditors are also required to report if, in their opinion:

(*a*)   proper accounting records have not been kept;

(*b*)   proper returns from branches have not been received;

(*c*)   the balance sheet and profit and loss accounts are not in agreement with the accounting records and returns.

If the audit report is silent with regard to these matters, then the auditors are indicating that there are no material problems in respect of these requirements. It is the duty of the directors of a company to prepare financial statements which give a true and fair view of the state of affairs of the company and of its results, but it is the auditor's responsibility to form an independent opinion on those financial statements.

In the UK auditors have a duty to carry out their work in accordance with auditing standards issued by the Auditing Practices Board. Those standards require that the audit is adequately planned and performed so as to obtain all the information and explanations considered necessary and in order to provide sufficient evidence that the financial statements are free from material misstatement whether caused by fraud or any other irregularity or error.

Financial controls

5.3   As mentioned elsewhere in this book, hotels vary considerably in their size and complexity and also in the group structures into which they fit. The system of financial controls in a large hotel is likely to be very different from that in a small, owner-managed hotel. A large hotel will very often be, in effect, a large and complex set of complementary businesses, including room lettings, restaurant services, bar services, laundry services and possibly a range of in-house shops. An hotel which is part of a large group of other hotels is also likely to be subject to an internal audit function and vigorous controls imposed and checked from a central head office. It can therefore be seen that the work carried out by the external auditor will vary considerably to suit the circumstances of an individual hotel. Indeed, a small hotel which is part of a large group may not even be visited by the external auditors every year as it may not be of sufficient significance to the group of which it forms a part.

A typical approach to an audit is summarised in the diagram overleaf.

Audit planning

5.4   The standards which govern the auditing profession require the auditor to properly plan his work. An auditor will obviously also wish to plan the audit in detail for reasons of efficiency. This is also a useful opportunity to discuss with the senior management or the proprietor of the hotel their concerns so that these can be usefully incorporated into the audit plan. The extent of planning will vary according to the size and structure of the hotel and also whether it is independent or exists within a group. The audit plan should, however, always include as a minimum the following:

(*a*)   background to the company and the individual hotel(s);

(*b*)   general economic/sectoral information;

(*c*)   services provided by the hotel;

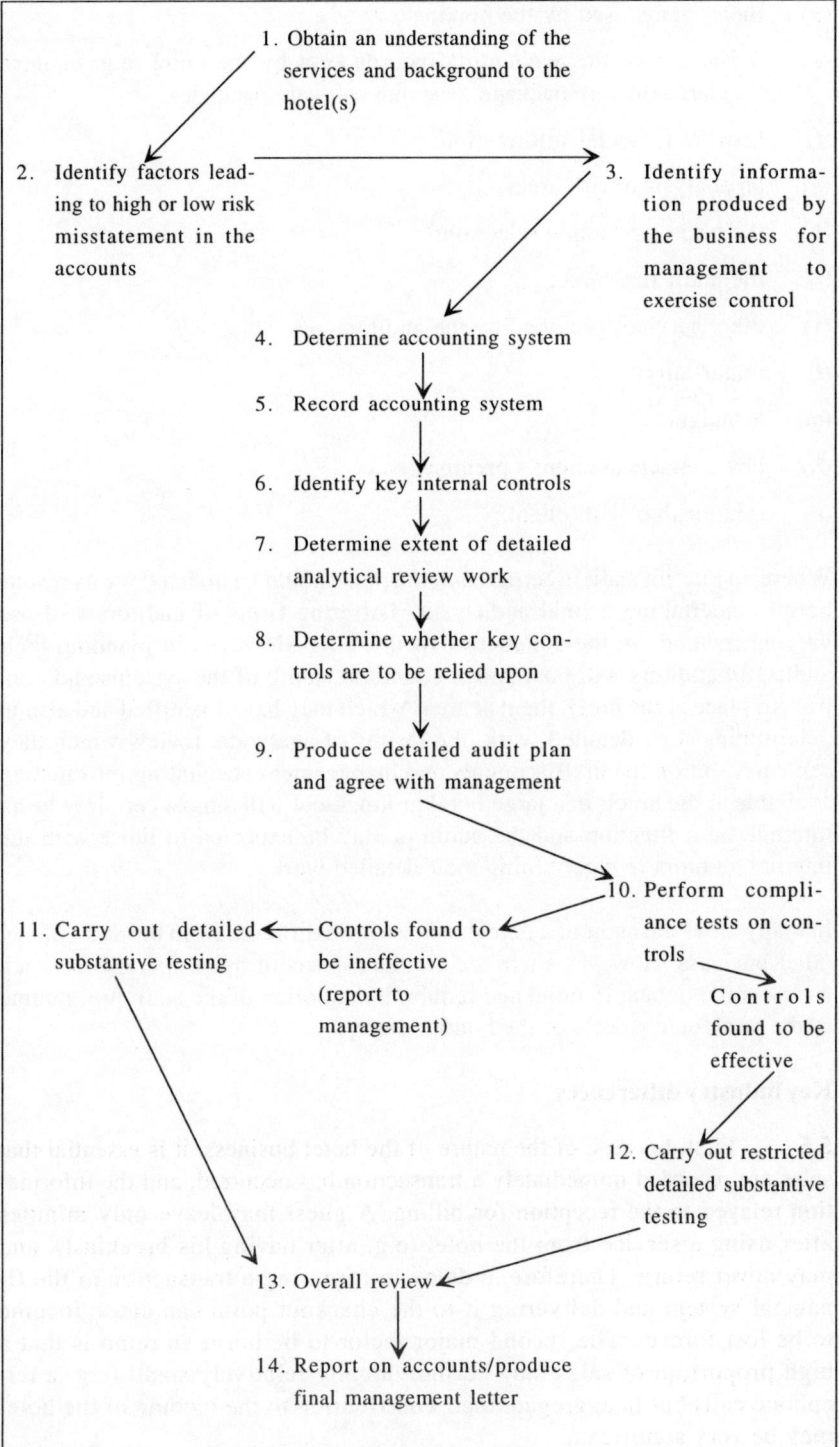

1. Obtain an understanding of the services and background to the hotel(s)

2. Identify factors leading to high or low risk misstatement in the accounts

3. Identify information produced by the business for management to exercise control

4. Determine accounting system

5. Record accounting system

6. Identify key internal controls

7. Determine extent of detailed analytical review work

8. Determine whether key controls are to be relied upon

9. Produce detailed audit plan and agree with management

10. Perform compliance tests on controls

Controls found to be ineffective (report to management)

11. Carry out detailed substantive testing

Controls found to be effective

12. Carry out restricted detailed substantive testing

13. Overall review

14. Report on accounts/produce final management letter

(*d*)   the systems used by the hotel;

(*e*)   the nature of the accounting records kept by the hotel (e.g. manual, standard software package, bespoke software package);

(*f*)   historic financial information;

(*g*)   an analysis of risk areas;

(*h*)   the basis for sample selection;

(*j*)   the audit timetable;

(*k*)   other services provided by the auditor;

(*l*)   materiality;

(*m*)   a budget;

(*n*)   key contacts at client's premise; and

(*o*)   relationship with client.

Where an interim audit is carried out, the plan should be updated for its results before undertaking a final audit visit. Differing firms of auditors will use varying methods in the conduct of their audits. However, in planning their audits, all auditors will take into account the nature of the systems and controls in place at the hotel, the risk areas which they have identified and also in determining their detailed work, the results of analytical review which they can carry out on the draft accounts and management accounting information available at the hotel. In a large hotel group, there will almost certainly be an internal audit function and the auditors may be expected to liaise with the internal auditors in determining their detailed work.

In many areas the audit of a hotel business is no different from the audit of any other business. However, there are certain aspects of hotel operations which are essential to bear in mind and require the tailoring of the audit programme to the particular aspects of the hotel industry.

Key industry differences

5.5   First, because of the nature of the hotel business, it is essential that sales are recorded immediately a transaction has occurred, and the information relayed to the reception for billing. A guest may leave only minutes after using a service from the hotel (e.g. after having his breakfast), and may never return. Therefore, a delay in capturing a transaction in the financial system and delivering it to the checkout point can cause income to be lost forever. The second major factor to be borne in mind is that a high proportion of sales may be individually relatively small (e.g. a telephone call) but in aggregate their contribution to the income of the hotel may be very significant.

Audit planning checklist

5.6   The following checklist gives an overview of the types of information and analyses that should be available to the auditors, to ensure the audit is completed as quickly and easily as possible. The checklist is not exhaustive, and hotels should discuss detailed requirements with their individual auditors.

Account area	Source documentation	Analyses required	Client staff who should be available to talk to the auditors
Fixed assets	Fixed asset register List of acquisitions in the year List of disposals in the year Details of the last professional valuation	Reconciliation of registers to the nominal ledger and draft accounts	Staff involved in updating the fixed asset register
Investments	As above for the investment register	As above	As above for the investment register
Stock	Stock records including the stocktake sheets	Reconciliation of the stock records to the nominal ledger and draft accounts	Staff responsible for stock, e.g. bar manager, restaurant manager, housekeeper
	Provision details	Breakdown of any provision for obsolescence damaged stock etc.	As above
Debtors and income	Customer bills Other invoices raised Aged debtors listing	Reconciliation of debtors listing to nominal ledger and draft accounts	Credit control and sales ledger staff
	Bad debt provision	Breakdown of bad debt provision	
	Schedule of prepayments	Analysis of prepayments by type/supplier	
Cash and Bank	Bank statements and cash book Details of any overdraft/loan agreements and covenants	Reconciliation of balances to bank statements and to the nominal ledger and draft accounts	Bank and finance staff
Creditors and costs	All purchase invoices received in the year	Schedules for specific disclosure items such as hire of plant and machinery etc.	Finance and purchase ledger staff

Account area	Source documentation	Analyses required	Client staff who should be available to talk to the auditors
	An aged creditors listing	Reconciliation of the creditors listing to the nominal ledger and draft accounts	
	A schedule of year-end accruals	Breakdown of accruals by type or supplier	
Share capital and reserves	Schedule of movements in equity and reserves in the year Company secretarial information	Reconciliation of information to the nominal ledger and draft accounts	Company secretarial and finance staff
Payroll costs	All payroll information including contracts of employment, pay listings etc. Schedule of directors emoluments	Reconciliation of the payroll information to the nominal ledger and draft accounts	Personnel and finance staff

Ascertaining and recording the system of accounting and controls

5.7   The auditor is required to ascertain the system recording and processing transactions and to assess its adequacy for the preparation of financial statements. This record may be performed in a number of ways from simple narrative notes to detailed flow charts. It may be expected that any large hotel would have procedures manuals and organisation charts including much of the information which the auditor requires. In addition where there is an internal audit function, the auditors may be able to liaise to obtain much of the information they need from the internal auditors.

Of course, as part of the auditor's work, they will need to ensure that the systems that they have been told exist, do actually function as described in reality. To this end, they will normally carry out a series of 'walk through tests' to ensure that this is the case at the record stage. These consist of tracing a transaction from its initial record point to its final realisation as cash and inclusion in the records, or vice versa. Having recorded and considered the system, this knowledge can then be built into the audit plan. Controls on which the auditor intends to rely will be further tested as part of the detailed audit work. Where the systems are found to be different from those originally envisaged, the audit plan will need to be varied accordingly. The auditor will be looking particularly for authorisation controls relating to transactions, proper segregation of duties, controls to ensure the completeness of recorded transactions, physical controls over the assets of the company and the extent of management supervision and control. The nature and strength of these aspects contained within the system will be used by the auditor in determining the detailed work carried out.

Computer financial systems

5.8   Computer systems within the hotel industry vary considerably in the degree of centralisation involved.

Most of the major chains use centralised reservations systems, where customers can organise hotel booking for any hotel in the chain by calling one central number. There is no clear trend in the use of off-the-shelf or internal systems, though internal systems are slightly more common.

The accounting systems used also include a split of off-the-shelf and own systems. Where off-the-shelf packages are used they usually have had bespoke adjustments to tailor them to the needs of a hotel operation.

The degree of centralisation varies throughout the sector, depending on the ownership and operational structure of the chain, e.g. companies operating franchised chains, have accounting systems operating on a local not central level.

As part of his exercise in understanding the client's systems, the auditor should ensure he fully understands the computer systems in operation. This will enable him to design detailed audit-testing that makes the best use of the management and accounting information available to him.

Internal control

5.9   Within any organisation management will have organised the systems they use to include various checks and review procedures. This 'control environment' will be evaluated by the auditor. The auditor assesses the control environment in order to understand the framework in which the accounting and internal control systems are designed and implemented and to help identify inherent risks which might increase the risk of misstatement in financial statements. The specific objectives include the following:

(*a*)   to assess whether the control environment is conducive to the maintenance of a reliable system of accounting and control procedures;

(*b*)   to assess the incentives and opportunities for intentional misrepresentation or distortion of the financial statements by management or others;

71

(c)   to determine management's ability to make the judgements and estimates that are necessary in the preparation of financial statements;

(d)   to assess whether management has sufficient reliable information for the effective control of the business, and whether it is using such information effectively;

(e)   to identify the key indicators, reports and procedures that management uses to control the business and determine which may be relevant for audit purposes; and

(f)   to identify the impact of specific control environmental factors, both favourable and unfavourable, on the risk of material misstatement in the financial statements.

The auditor uses the knowledge of the control environment to plan the audit strategy and the extent of substantive testing. This is because:

(i)   an effective control will indicate that it may be more efficient for the auditor to concentrate on testing the controls over particular accounts rather than undertaking extensive substantive testing;

(ii)   even if the auditor feels extensive testing of controls is not appropriate he might still conclude that the risk of material misstatement of account balances was generally lower because of the existence of positive control features for which there is appropriate evidence, and that therefore the auditor would need to obtain less comfort from substantive tests;

(iii) a poor control environment will lead the auditor to conclude that controls could not contribute significantly to the prevention or detection of material misstatement in the financial statements. In such cases it would generally not be efficient to make an extended assessment of controls and the auditor would derive audit assurance primarily from substantive tests;

(iv)   a weak control environment is a strong indicator of inherent risks of misstatement arising from fraud or error. Consequently, the auditor should be alert (and alert management) to factors identified during the assessment which affect the risk of material misstatement arising from fraud or error.

Internal controls will be required as part of the prudent management of any hotel. However, their extent will vary with the size and nature of the hotel and management's judgement of the cost/benefit derived from them.

Listed companies are required to comply with the Cadbury Committee's Code of Best Practice (published in December 1992). This includes the requirement for the directors to report on the company's/groups systems of internal financial control. This statement is required to be reviewed by the auditors.

The kind of controls which typically may be expected to exist in an hotel are summarised as follows for illustrative purposes (note that this list cannot be considered exhaustive).

Example of controls in the hotel environment

5.10

(*a*)   *General*

(i)   Regular production of operating reports covering segmental analysis of trading compared with budget and prior year.

(ii)   Regular production of cash flow reports, both current and projected.

(iii)   Segregation of duties between those who record transactions and those who handle assets and incur liabilities.

(iv)   In a large hotel, internal audit.

(v)   Effective review and procedures for action where matters arise from the above.

(*b*)   *Revenue*

(i)   Controls over rooms:

(A)   Systems to ensure all arrivals and departures are notified by reception to those responsible for maintaining the guest's ledger.

(B)   Housekeeper's report produced and reconciled to the accounting records by independent staff.

(C)   Fixed room rates used with any variance written authorisation by senior management.

(D)   Room income reconciled to theoretical maximum income and variances investigated.

(E)   Fixed advance payment procedures.

(F)   Controls to ensure it is difficult for guests to leave without paying (e.g. holding of passports, credit card slip, deposit, and guest ledger credit limits).

(ii)   Controls over food and drink sales:

(A)   Pre-numbered waiters' pads.

(B)   Secure control of waiters' pads.

(C)   Segregation of kitchen staff and cashier duties etc.

      (D)   Reconciliation/test checking of orders to billings.

      (E)   Test checking of menu prices to bills.

      (F)   Reconciliation of liquor stock transfers between departments.

      (G)   Review of food/drink margins to known/expected mark-ups.

      (H)   Portion controls.

  (iii) Controls over telephone revenue:

      (A)   Metering of calls.

      (B)   Control of resetting of meters.

      (C)   Reconciliation of income to cost/margins.

      (D)   Payphone takings reconciled to metered calls.

  (iv) Controls over special events:

      (A)   Control diary of events.

      (B)   Reconciliation of agreed attendees to headcount at the actual event.

      (C)   Controls over meals/buffet issued to the event.

      (D)   Reconciliation of liquor allocated/ordered for the event to that consumed.

      (E)   Agreed PAYE procedures for any casual labour required for a special event.

  (iv) Controls over bookings:

      (A)   Reservation deposits listing agreed to guest ledger.

      (B)   Control accounts and reconciliation of travel agent's commissions.

(*c*)   Cash receipts:

  (i) Till reconciliations reviewed by senior independent personnel.

  (ii) Safe facilities available.

(*d*)   Floats:

  (i) Test counts.

  (ii) Imprest system and regular reconciliations.

  (iii) Authorisation control procedures for varying level of payments.

(*e*)   Receivables:

  (i) Authorisation controls over transfers from guest to debtors ledger.

    (ii) Segregation of duties between debtors ledger clerk(s) and those responsible for receipts/banking of cash and cheques.

    (iii) Review of aged debtors ledger by senior official.

    (iv) Credit limits on guest ledger and debtors ledger.

    (v) Authorisation of bad debts write-offs (and review of write-offs) by a senior official.

    (vi) A record of 'walk-outs'.

(*f*)   Operating assets such as linen, cutlery:

    (i) Periodic stock counts.

    (ii) Review of costs on a periodic basis with a clear system of reporting and investigation for abnormal losses.

(*g*)   Food and liquor:

    (i) Authorisation by a senior official of purchase orders.

    (ii) Agreement of receipts to orders and checking of goods inward for quality and quantity.

    (iii) Secure storerooms.

    (iv) Issuing procedures to ensure first in first out and clear date marking of perishable items.

    (v) Standard written requisitioning procedures and documents.

    (vi) Inventory counts and margin reviews by senior personnel.

    (vii) Monthly review of slow moving items.

    (viii) Control of opened bottles.

(*h*)   Payroll:

    (i) Written contracts of employment.

    (ii) Written staff scheduling plans.

    (iii) Written advance authorisation of overtime required (which is reconciled to overtime claimed).

    (iv) Time records for hourly paid staff.

    (v) Standard rates of pay.

    (vi) Review of holidays.

    (vii) Signature required for receipt of cash wages.

    (viii) Regular procedures for verifying status of staff who say they are self-employed.

(ix) Written Tronc system procedures (see 5.12 below).

(*j*)   Laundry:

(i) Secure storage control.

(ii) Reconciliation of cleaning invoices to housekeeping records (below).

(iii) Inventory procedures, to include regular counts, written instructions and reporting/review procedures.

Analytical review

5.11   'Analytical review' is the term used to describe techniques of varying complexity involving the consideration of comparisons and relationships between data (not necessarily just accounting data). Widely applicable procedures include the following:

(*a*)   analysing the relationship between items of financial data (e.g. between sales and the cost of the sales);

(*b*)   considering the relationship between financial and non-financial data, e.g. employee costs and employee headcount;

(*c*)   comparing actual data with predicted data (based on expected relationships or trends);

(*d*)   comparing results for the latest financial period with earlier periods;

(*e*)   comparing data for one entity with that from a comparable entity or averages for the sector;

(*f*)   investigating and comparing the results and explanations with other sources of audit evidence;

(*g*)   investigating unexpected results arising from the type of work outlined above and substantiating explanations.

Management accounts

5.12   All well-managed hotels will produce management accounts which will be produced from the same prime records as the statutory accounts. Most of these management accounts will be based around the 'Uniform system of accounts for Hotels,' or the 'Standard system of Hotel accounting'. These are standard methods of reporting income and costs which are widespread throughout the industry. An example of the kind of management information which these systems produce is shown overleaf. It should be noted that more detailed reports will usually support the summary statement shown here and will be distributed to the relevant managers.

Summary Operating Statement

	Month				Year to date			
	Budget	%	Actual	%	Budget	%	Actual	%
REVENUE Rooms Food and beverages Minor operated Depts. Other income TOTAL REVENUE								
COST OF SALES Food and beverages Minor operated Depts. Other income TOTAL OF SALES								
PAYROLL AND RELATED EXPENSES Rooms Food and beverages Minor operated Depts. Other income TOTAL PAYROLL								
OTHER EXPENSES Rooms Food and beverages Minor operated Depts. Other income TOTAL OTHER EXPENSES								
DEPARTMENTAL OPERATING PROFITS Rooms Food and beverages Minor operated Depts. Other income TOTAL DEPART-MENTAL OPERAT-ING PROFITS								
UNDISTRIBUTED OVERHEADS Administration and general marketing Property operation Energy TOTAL OVERHEAD EXPENSES								
PROFIT BEFORE MANAGMENT FEES AND FIXED CHARGES Management fees Rent, property tax and insurance								
NET OPERATING PROFIT Depreciation Interest								
NET PROFIT (BEFORE) TAXATION								

5.13 *The Audit of Hotels*

The auditor should be able to make considerable use of such management accounting information in carrying out analytical review work. It is generally accepted that the auditor of an hotel can gain considerable audit evidence from the review of key operating ratios and comparisons with budgets and prior year results, together with industry-wide information.

Examples of analytical review tests

5.13   Typical examples of analytical review tests are as follows.

(a)   Consideration of the previous year's profit and loss accounts with those of the current year, bearing in mind known industry conditions and results from other establishments.

(b)   Occupancy tests – the number of rooms available for letting in the hotel through the year should be readily ascertainable. It should also be possible to obtain the room rates applied during the year. Although this may be complicated by discount arrangements and rates varying between rooms, it should be possible to compute maximum room sales figures on a monthly basis and to compare the actual monthly figures to these maximum figures to give a percentage occupancy rate. An example of an occupancy test is given below.

Room Rate	No of Rooms	Days	Maximum Revenue
£			£
100	100	30	300,000
120	50	30	180,000
			480,000

If actual room income is £350,000 this implies an occupancy rate of 73 per cent

$$\text{i.e. } \frac{350,000 \times 100}{480,000}$$

This can be compared to the results for the previous year, published statistics for hotels within the same category, or if applicable other hotels within the same group and with views gained from discussion with management.

The industry ratios for occupancy percentages depend heavily on the geographical location and the category of hotel involved. Hotels classified as 3 or 4 star, which have a high level of business guests tend to have an even pattern of occupancy from period to period. In contrast small B&B's can have wide fluctuations depending on group bookings and local events.

On average occupancy ratios fall within 60 to 65 per cent. However, there are large regional variations, with occupancy rates in London averaging 70 to 75 per cent. In contrast provincial hotels average 50 to 55 per cent occupancy, year on year. There is not a marked difference in occupancy rates between large and small hotels. Although large hotels (over 150 rooms) in general have higher occupancy rates, the difference is only in the region of 1 to 2 per cent, compared to hotels with less than 100 rooms.

It can also be compared with other records such as the housekeeper's records. If these statistics are in line with expectations and valid comparisons, the auditor can draw considerable comfort from the results of this testing.

(c) Consideration of seasonal trends e.g. monthly levels of occupancy with prior periods/budgets. Unexpected changes may indicate misstatements in the financial statements.

The importance of seasonal trends varies considerably with the location and type of hotel involved. For example, small seaside hotels with 5 to 10 rooms may have minimal bookings in the winter but be booked up throughout the high season. In contrast large hotels that rely on business or conference trade may not show a significant variation in trade month on month. The normal seasonal trade will also be affected by particular local events, such as the D Day celebrations in Portsmouth.

On average occupancy rates decline in January, after the Christmas rush. They then rise month on month peaking in July to September, which are the main holiday months.

These are averages for the industry as a whole, as the pattern for individual hotels will vary. Small hotels, relying on personal and holiday trade, will conform to the average pattern more than large business hotels.

Therefore, hotels in setting, and auditors in reviewing, budgeted or expected monthly income should consider all these factors. Not only will it highlight reasons for overall occupancy changes but may also identify future marketing and publicity opportunities.

(d) Food sales – the cost of sales can be expressed as a percentage of revenue from sales

$$\text{i.e.} \quad \frac{\text{Cost of food}}{\text{Revenue from food}} \times 100$$

This can also be compared with prior year statistics and estimates obtained from conversations with management.

(e) Beverage sales – the ratio of the cost of sales over revenue from sales can be calculated and compared to prior year figures and management expectations.

(*f*)   Similar testing to (*c*) and (*d*) above can also be applied to other areas such as telephone revenue and laundry, if these are material.

(*g*)   Comparison of the number of debtor days outstanding i.e.

$$\frac{\text{debtors}}{\text{sales}} \times 365$$

at the close of a period compared to prior periods and averages during the period.

(*h*)   The number of creditor days outstanding at the period end.

(*j*)   Where stocks are significant again, the number of stock days.

In all cases where unexpected variances are noted, these should be discussed with management, and wherever possible, the auditor should substantiate any explanations given with supporting documentation.

Detailed testing

5.14   Having assessed the system, the controls operated within it, the risk associated with various activities and the results of analytical review, the auditor will be in position to design effective tests to support the audit opinion in the most efficient manner. These tests will broadly be of two kinds, as follows:

(*a*)   Compliance tests – these check that the controls recorded within the system are in fact being carried out. Where testing proves that these do exist and are carried out the auditor can reduce his second type of testing.

(*b*)   Substantive testing – these test transaction and asset balances.

Obviously, the balance and extent of these types of tests will depend on the nature and size of the hotel and the results of the previous work referred to above. Auditors do not, except in rare circumstances, vouch every transaction. They will adopt a variety of sampling techniques ranging from sophisticated statistically based methods to purely judgemental methods. In all cases they will endeavour to ensure that material balances and transaction streams are tested, but that there is no inherent bias in the samples they pick beyond considerations of materiality and risk.

Audit evidence

5.15   The general rule of auditing, is that third party external evidence is more useful than internal information produced by the hotel. Therefore it is important that hotels maintain files of all external documentation received.

For example, an hotel is showing accrued income for guests in residence at the year end. A good source of external evidence of the amount due is the notification of the amount charged from a travel agent.

Evidence from travel agents and tourist boards could also be used to validate other account figures such as trade debtors, commissions due, billing rates etc. Similarly bank statements and purchase invoices provide assurance for the cash, creditors and costs figures in the accounts.

The financial statements

5.16 The acceptable formats, contents and basis of preparation of the financial statements which the directors of a company are required to prepare and the auditors are required to report on are laid down in law. *Companies Act 1985* is the single most important piece of legislation pertaining to this. *Companies Act 1985* lays down formats for the statutory accounts and requires that the accounts so drawn up should give a 'true and fair' view. *Companies Act 1989* gave statutory recognition to the existence of accounting standards, principally through the insertion of a new section (*section 256*) into *Companies Act 1985*.

The entity responsible for these standards in the UK is the Accounting Standards Board ('ASB'). It issues 'Financial Reporting Standards' (FRSs). Subsequent to its formation it adopted the existing 'Statements of Standard Accounting Practice' which had been issued by the councils of various major accountancy bodies in the UK following proposals developed by what was effectively the ASB's predecessor, the Accounting Standard Committee (ASC). In addition to FRSs the ASB also issues pronouncements in a shorter timescale relating to issues which are considered to require more rapid guidance. They are generally issued as Urgent Issues Task Force Abstracts ('UITFs'). Accounting standards and UITFs are applicable to financial statements that are intended to give a true and fair view and should thus be adopted in the preparation of all financial statements except for rare instances where their adoption would conflict with requirements to show a true and fair view. If this is the case UITF 7 requires full details of the effect and reasons for the departure to be given.

Audit testing

5.17 Different firms of auditors will approach the audit in slightly differing ways, although the methods used and standards followed should be the same. In reaching the overall audit opinion as to whether or not the financial statements give a true and fair view, and have been properly prepared in accordance with *Companies Act 1985* the auditor will typically set a number of sub-objectives around which appropriate tests are designed and conclusions drawn. The actual testing performed will depend upon the results of the consideration of controls and analytical review outlined in 5.11 above.

The table which follows shows examples of typical objectives and examples of testing which might be chosen to meet the objectives. This table is for illustrative purposes only and neither the list of objectives nor appropriate tests should be considered as exhaustive, or appropriate in all circumstances. In all cases the auditor will be seeking assurance as to the completeness, accuracy and validity of all figures in the accounts.

Example of overall objective	Example tests
Intangible fixed assets are owned and stated at the proper amount.	Review balances against prior year/ expectations. Check (sample of) additions to supporting documentation. Consider basis of valuation/ amortisation and test check calculations. Agree balances to nominal ledger. Check title (e.g. of trade marks). Consider disclosure.
Fixed assets comprise only and all expenditure of a capital nature.	Check a sample of additions to supporting documentation/ authorisation/physical existence. Ensure finance leases are accounted for in accordance with SSAP21. Check a sample of disposals for correct accounting treatment and backing documentation. Review minutes/order books etc. for possible capital commitments requiring disclosure at the year end.
Fixed assets exist at the year end and are properly valued and categorised.	Review balances against prior year/ expectations.

Example of overall objective	Example tests
	Physically vouch a sample of brought forward fixed assets.
	Review basis of depreciation charge and ensure it is correct and consistent with prior years.
	Check inclusion in the accounts of any valuations.
	Examine evidence of title.
Investments are owned, exist at the year end, and are properly valued/ categorised.	Check a sample of additions to backing documentation and ensure correct categorisation and authorisation.
	Check a sample of investments to ensure legal title is held.
	Ensure all relevant valuations are recorded in the accounts.
	Consider adequacy of provision for diminutions in value.
	Review against prior year/ expectations.
Income from investments and profits/losses on sales are correctly accounted for.	Check a sample of sales of investments and ensure correct accounting treatment.
	Ensure all dividends, bonus issues, interest payments etc. are properly recorded and accounted for.
Stock exists, is owned and all stocks are included in the accounts.	Attend stocktake to ensure adequate and effective stocktaking procedures are applied.

Example of overall objective	Example tests
	Select a sample of goods at stocktake to check whether all stocks are recorded in the accounts.
Stocks are properly valued.	Select a sample of year end stock and trace to purchase documentation to ensure the cost of stock is correct. Trace a sample of year end stock to subsequent sale to ensure adequate provision has been made for any value of stock where net realisable value is lower.
Debtors included in the accounts are not overstated and represent valid and recoverable amounts.	Review the overall level of debtors and compare all material balances with prior years and expectations. Consider debtor days. Consider controls in operation and if appropriate check they are operating. Test check calculation of prepayment balances. Check/reconcile the debtors ledger to the general ledger control account. Circularise a sample of debtors to confirm outstanding balances. Review level of cash received after the year end to ensure adequate provision has been made against bad or doubtful debts. Review a sample of credit notes issued post-year end to ensure adequate provision has been made.

Example of overall objective	Example tests
Sales are recorded in the correct period and are therefore neither understated nor overstated.	Check a sample of sales invoices raised around the year end to ensure correct accounting for cut-off has occurred.
All sales are included in the accounts in the proper amount and sales are therefore not understated.	Review the current system for transacting and recording sales and ensure it is correctly documented and understood.
	Record controls in operation, consider adequacy and whether they should be tested. Review balances against prior year/expectations.
	Select a sample of sales transactions and ensure that invoices are correctly raised and recorded in the nominal ledger and control accounts.
	Select a sample of credit notes issued during the year and ensure they are bona fide. Review investments and check to backing evidence of title.
Investments in group and other related enterprises exist, are owned and stated at the proper amount.	Review investments and check to evidence of title.
	Ensure valuation of investments is reasonable and basis of valuation properly disclosed.
Amounts due to/from group and other related enterprises are properly recorded.	Ensure group balances are agreed by the other enterprises' records and are fully recoverable.
	Ensure all trading between group companies is on an arm's length basis and/or consider disclosure.

Example of overall objective	Example tests
Bank balances are correctly recorded and transactions not covered elsewhere are valid.	Obtain bank letters in respect of all accounts held in the period, and agree to bank reconciliations. Consider controls in operation, their adequacy and whether they should be tested. Review balances against prior year's expectations. Reconcile all year end balances to cash book/nominal ledger. Review petty cash expenditure for reasonableness. If material test count petty cash balances.
All creditors are included in the accounts and creditors are therefore not understated.	Check/reconcile the purchase ledger to the creditors control account in the nominal ledger. Agree a sample of year end creditors to third party confirmation e.g. supplier statements. Consider circularising creditors. Ensure adequate provision exists for payroll expenses and VAT liability. Review all sundry creditors and accruals and compare with prior years.
Cost of goods sold and expenses are recorded in the correct period and are therefore neither understated nor overstated.	Check a sample of purchase invoices either side of the year end to ensure correct cut off has occurred. Test completeness of creditors by reviewing post year end invoices, payments and other transactions.

Example of overall objective	Example tests
	Ensure that all hire purchase and finance lease agreements are correctly accounted for. Check that any balances on directors' accounts are properly stated.
All necessary entries are made in the accounts in respect of taxation and these are properly stated.	Analyse and vouch movements in the nominal ledger tax accounts in the period. Review and check tax computations.
Entries in statutory registers and minutes are reflected in the accounts and vice versa. Registers have been kept and returns made as required by *Companies Act*.	Inspect the minutes and note relevant items for cross reference to the accounts. Ensure that minutes include all statutory requirements (e.g. re-appointment of directors at AGM etc). Cross check entries in statutory registers to disclosure in the accounts. Ensure that the Registrar has been notified of any change required by statute.
Contingent liabilities and commitments are identified and properly disclosed.	Review bank letters for contingencies and commitments. Consider requesting client to obtain direct confirmations from lawyers. Discuss any further liabilities with client such as threatened litigation, and consider disclosure. Review balances against prior years and expectations.

Example of overall objective	Example tests
Expenditure relating to payroll costs is not overstated.	Reconcile the nominal ledger to the payroll. Test check detailed PAYE/NIC computations/authorisation of payroll costs/existence of employees.
Entries in the nominal ledger and trial balance have been subject to audit and opening/closing balances agree with accounts.	Consider disclosure requirements. Review the Trial Balance and Nominal Ledger to ensure all entries are from sources subjected to audit tests. Agree all opening balances to prior year accounts and ensure all closing balances per the Trial Balance agree to the Nominal Ledger. Agree the extraction of Financial Statements from trial balance.
To ensure the financial statements are fairly presented and comply with the *Companies Acts* and Standard Accounting Practice.	Check cross-references within the financial statements and consider whether other reports, such as the Director's Report, are consistent with the information therein. Check casting. Cross reference all items in the financial statements to working papers. Complete disclosure checklists. Consider post balance sheet events and validity of going concern assumptions.

Accounting policies and methods

5.18 The auditor is required to assess whether the directors have used appropriate accounting policies in drawing up the accounts. As outlined in 5.17 these should be in line with financial reporting standards issued by the accountancy bodies. In many cases this is fairly straightforward and the standards applied in the hotel industry are similar to those applied in industry at large. However, there are a number of areas where the hotel industry presents specific problems. The paragraphs which follow outline the most significant of these.

Depreciation of freehold and leasehold buildings

5.19 Legislation and SSAP 12 require that depreciation is provided on freehold and leasehold buildings:

> 'Buildings are no different from other fixed assets in that they have a useful economic life, albeit usually significantly longer than that of other types of assets. They should, therefore, be depreciated, having regard to the same criteria.' (Para 24, SSAP 12).

The management of many hotels and hotel groups consider that in reality the depreciation of their buildings is not material unless they are held on relatively short leases, as they are maintained to high standards.

Forte plc had some discussions into problems with the Financial Reporting Review Panel with respect to their implementation of this view. The 1991 accounting policy was as follows.

> 'Depreciation: No depreciation is provided on freehold properties or properties on leases with 20 years and over to run at the balance sheet date or on integral fixed plant. It is the Group's practice to maintain these assets in a continual state of sound repair and to extend and make improvements thereto from time to time and accordingly the directors consider that the lives of these assets are so long and residual values so high that depreciation is insignificant. All properties held on leases of less than 20 years are amortised over the unexpired term except where the anticipated renewal of the lease is sufficiently certain so that a longer depreciation period is appropriate. Depreciation is provided on all other tangible fixed assets on a straight line bais over 10 – 15 years for plant and machinery and 4 –10 years for furniture and equipment.'

In 1992, the Financial Reporting Review Panel examined these accounts and in particular considered the appropriateness of the above policy. They subsequently reported that they were satisfied by the explanations provided by the directors and there was no cause for further action, but the directors agreed to clarify two points in the next accounts:

(*a*)   that their appraisal of residual values was based on prices prevailing at the time of acquisition or subsequent valuation of the property in question (as specified by SSAP 12, para 12); and

(*b*)   that they would provide for any future permanent diminution in value through the profit and loss account.

These changes were duly made, as shown in this extract from the 1992 accounts.

'Depreciation: No depreciation is provided on freehold properties or properties on leases with 20 years and over to run at the balance sheet date or on integral fixed plant. It is the Group's practice to maintain these assets in a continual state of sound repair and to extend and make improvements thereto from time to time and accordingly the directors consider that the lives of these assets are so long and residual values, **based on prices prevailing at the time of acquisition or subsequent revaluation,** are so high that depreciation is insignificant. **Any permanent diminution in the value of such properties is charged to the profit and loss account as appropriate**. All properties held on leases of less than 20 years are amortised over the unexpired term except where the anticipated renewal of the lease is sufficiently certain so that a longer depreciation period is appropriate. Depreciation is provided on all other tangible fixed assets on a straight line basis over 10 –15 years for plant and machinery and 4 –10 years for furniture and equipment.'

The accounting policy is the same in 1993 accounts.

A further example of this type of accounting policy is shown below.

'No depreciation is provided in respect of freehold and long leasehold hotels, or on hotels with leases having 20 years or more to run at the balance sheet date, as it is considered that the length of lives and residual values of these buildings, which are assessed at each revaluation, are such that any depreciation would be immaterial. Any permanent diminutions in value below cost of such buildings are charged to profit and loss account. Hotels held under leases of less than 20 years are amortised over the unexpired term except where the anticipated renewal of the lease is sufficiently certain so that a longer depreciation period is appropriate. Other freehold and leasehold buildings are written off over a period of 50 years or estimated length of life of the building, or the lease, whichever is less.' (Extract from Ladbroke Accounts 1993).

Valuation of hotels

5.20   *Companies Act 1985* allows fixed assets to be carried at a valuation and many hotels are included in accounts at such a valuation. The hotel industry has suffered from sharp cyclical up and down turns. In addition there are difficulties in disassociating the 'bricks and mortar' (see 4.21 above) of an hotel from 'goodwill', i.e. the profitability associated with a good reputation. The problem of valuing hotels has been highlighted in a number of very public cases (e.g. *Queen's Moat House plc*) where professionally prepared valuations performed by different firms of chartered surveyors have produced radically different values. In response to such cases, The Royal Institute of Chartered Surveyors (RICS) have issued a New Red Book which will be of particular assistance to the hotel surveyor. The British Association of Hotel Accountants (see 4.21 above) produced a practice statement on this subject in 1993. Any reader of a hotel company's accounts would be advised to look closely at this area in assessing the financial strength of that company.

The following example of an accounting policy relating to the valuation of hotel properties has been extracted from Resort Hotels plc accounts 1993.

'The trading properties are revalued by independent valuers at the end of every financial period and any temporary difference thus arising is adjusted through the revaluation reserve unless this would result in an overall deficit on that reserve in which case the difference is taken to the profit and loss account on the grounds of prudence. Where a diminution in value is regarded as permanent, the diminution is charged to the profit and loss account to the extent that it does not relate to an existing revaluation surplus which arose on the same asset'.

Pre-opening expenses

5.21   In addition to normal construction expenses, hotels typically incur large costs before trading commences and these are often separately identified in the accounts as 'pre-opening expenses'. They should not be confused with formation expenses (i.e. the legal expenses associated with setting up any company). However, where they relate to expenditure that is normally considered to be of a revenue nature, because of the benefits they provide to future periods they may be treated as deferred revenue expenditure. All types of these pre-opening expenses may be capitalised and written off over a period of time, the duration being subject to the company's accounting policy. A period of five years is considered an industry norm, though many companies prefer to spread these costs over the first two or three years of operation, since subsequent to this period operating revenues and expenses will have stabilised. There are four main categories of these expenses.

Set up expenses

From the time that a new hotel is structurally substantially completed, but not open to the public, the following will be necessary:

(*a*)   staff will require training;

(*b*)   staff will have to be employed to stock the hotel with linen, cutlery, crockery, glasses, etc;

(c)   the manager, plus the key staff, may be required on the premises months before opening, to supervise (*a*) and (*b*) and to establish marketing arrangements;

(d)   administrative and accounting systems will have to be designed or purchased, implemented and tested;

(e)   the above activities also incur expenditure such as food and beverage for staff, stationery, utility charges, insurance, and rates.

Promotional expenses

Prior to the official opening, there will most likely be a rehearsed opening. Complimentary guests such as VIPs, corporate account holders and tour and travel agent managers, may be invited to use the hotel services free of charge or at nominal cost.

This 'soft opening' may continue for several weeks until all problems are eliminated and staff can run the hotel smoothly. The official opening itself may incur additional advertising expenses in relation to special events and other publicity.

Expenses incurred during refitting and extension

While parts of the hotel are being refitted or redecorated, and are therefore not available for use, the costs being incurred in the hotel as a whole with respect to this are sometimes identified and capitalised.

Capitalisation of interest

In common with many developers, hotel companies very often capitalise interest costs up to the date of completion and opening of a hotel for business.

The example accounting policy set out below is extracted from the 1993 accounts of Forte plc and covers both pre-opening and interest expenses.

'Interest on capital employed on land awaiting development and on the construction and major redevelopment of hotels and restaurants and internal professional costs incurred until these enterprises start to trade are capitalised as part of the costs of construction. In addition, pre-opening and development expenses incurred up to the commencement of full trading are deferred and written off over five to ten years.'

Management letters

5.22   During the course of an audit, it is likely that the auditor will note weaknesses in controls or controls which do not appear to have been carried out properly. There are also likely to be discussions regarding the appropriateness of accounting policies and changes in standard practice anticipated or known to be effective in future periods. The auditor will wish to communicate these to management. These communications will generally take place by discussion during the audit, but it is common practice to record these points formally in a letter to management, though in certain circumstances an exchange of agreed meeting minutes may be considered the most efficient medium or record. Such reports are known by a variety of names (e.g. 'letters of weakness', 'post audit letter'), but they effectively all serve the same purpose. They can also form a useful medium for communicating matters which the auditor may feel could be commercially advantageous to the client. Indeed most firms of auditors would hope to identify such points to ensure that the audit is seen as being an 'added value' service. Management comments should be incorporated into the letter in order to provide a basis for checking agreed actions in the subsequent year's audit.

Appendix 1 provides a checklist detailing typical points that may be raised in an hotel management letter.

Special considerations for hotel audits

Lettings

5.23   The letting of rooms will invariably provide the largest source of income for an hotel. Billings are normally worked out in terms of what is generally known as 'the charge day'. This is normally a period of 24 hours from 12:00 pm. A stay straddling more than two charge days would normally be charged as two full days. However, it is often the case that the charge day is waived, for example on package deals. In performing analytical reviews (see 5.11 above), it will be necessary to understand the hotel's policy with respect to such arrangements. Some hotels also obtain income from 'day lets' (i.e. non-overnight lets). The auditor should be aware if these are occurring, since it could be possible for the room to be let for two charge days, i.e. the night and the day. A misappropriation of one of these may not therefore be highlighted as it would still appear that the occupancy was 100 per cent.

To try to ensure maximum occupancy, some large hotels deliberately over-book based on previous experience. As a result, occasionally customers will arrive for whom there are no rooms. The hotel may then incur what are known as 'boarding out costs'. These are the costs of putting the guests into another hotel. The controls surrounding this should be considered for the possibility of misappropriations. In addition, the boarding out costs should be offset against the income from the hotel guests (as the hotel is effectively not earning the income itself).

The auditor should be aware of the hotel's policy with regard to non-arrivals, i.e. does the guest lose his deposit or receive a refund of all or a percentage of the deposit? The auditor may wish to check that the policies are being adhered to and that controls are sufficiently strong to minimise the possibility of the misappropriation of deposits for non-arrivers.

There is always some risk in a hotel that a guest will simply walk out without paying ('walk-outs'). Several methods may be used to try and minimise this risk including controls over the guests' luggage being taken out, mandatory deposits, blank copies of the credit card being kept as security, holding of passports and/or credit limits on the guests' ledger. Write offs in the guest and/ or debtor ledger may give some indication of the strength of the hotel's controls in this area.

Breakfasts

In many hotels, bed and breakfast is offered as a joint service, i.e. breakfast comes automatically with an overnight booking. Guests may not actually take breakfast. Therefore it is possible for staff to sell such breakfasts without any apparent anomaly in takings. Variances in the number of customers taking the breakfast they have paid for may also distort the food margin. The auditor should also be aware of the hotel's policy with regard to providing food to staff, as this may also have an effect on the gross food margin.

Bar sales

With respect to bar income, the auditor is largely dependent on the comparison of turnover figures and cost of sales for periods where data is available. If turnover from this sector is significant, the hotel should use independent stocktakers. Cost of sales can be compiled from opening stock plus purchases less sales equals closing stock. However, there are many ways to manipulate the formula so that no apparent anomalies occur, e.g. staff selling drinks supplied by themselves or topping up bottles. Any unexpected variations in turnover should therefore be investigated vigorously. Till roll reconciliations should also be carried out. It should also be noted that in particular where tobacco sales are taken through the same till, distortions of gross margins can occur.

Generally it should be possible to establish some pattern of consistency between occupancy levels and sales of other services and bar income. The exact relationship will be different for each individual hotel, and finance staff should use their internal management information to compare ratios on a weekly or monthly basis.

Factors which will influence an individual hotel's ratios include:

(a) the type of guest visiting – business travellers are more likely than holiday guests to use the laundry, bar services, restaurant etc.;

(b) other services offered by the hotel – hotels with acclaimed restaurants are likely to have higher bar sales as guests remain in the hotel complex during the evenings;

(c)   location of the hotel – hotels in isolated locations have higher bar and restaurant income, due to the lack of alternative facilities.

Special events

Many hotels earn significant income from banqueting and conferences and this may be a material transaction stream which the auditor needs to consider. It may be appropriate to examine the income and expenses associated with some individual banquets or conferences. The auditor would probably wish to check correspondence relating to the banquet and entries in the functions diary, together with charges from other departments to ensure the income and expenditure on the conference appears to be reasonable and that margins earned are reasonable. Banqueting and conferences typically involve the hiring of significant casual labour and the PAYE controls exercised here may need to be reviewed.

Rental income

Large hotels often lease or rent space e.g. to jewellers shops or hairdressing salons (see 5.11 above). The auditor will probably approach this income by way of analytical review and obtain a list of such premises and compare them to the previous year and agreements reconciling gross rents receivable to those actually received and investigating unusual variances.

Service charges and gratuities

In most hotels there will be significant levels of tips and gratuities or service charges levied by percentage additions to the guests' bills. Where these are collected centrally, such monies are paid over to staff by the hotel via the normal wages system or they may be dealt with by what is known as the 'Tronc Master'. A 'tronc' is the term given to a system whereby gratuities or service charges in a restaurant or hotel are paid into a central collection point and then paid out by one of the staff or management to, for example, the waiters and waitresses, bar staff etc. who have earned them. The person who makes the payments out (who may be known as the 'Tronc Master') is treated under PAYE law as the employer making a payment of emoluments (see 7.2 below). Treatment of service charges varies in different hotels. In some cases the staff are paid a fixed rate irrespective of the service charges collected, or the basic tariff prices may be inclusive of service charges and VAT. A tronc system pulls together all such amounts, which are then allocated to staff in agreed proportions often, on a time-worked basis. The Tronc Master is responsible for organising this, and is required to record all payments out and to deduct PAYE and account for this to the Inland Revenue. Service charges paid direct to the employee by the hotel will be subject to PAYE through the normal payroll. Where a tronc system is used, a hotel is not legally responsible for the tronc monies.

If a guest writes out a cheque including an additional sum as a tip then the hotel should pay the excess over to the Tronc Master where such a system is in place.

Insurance

There are a number of insurances considered particularly important or special to hotels and the auditors may wish to check that adequate and comprehensive insurance policies are in place. These should include:

(i)   building and contents (at replacement value);

(ii)   employers' liability insurance (including any part-time and casual staff, as well as full-time);

(iii)   link men insurance (covering commissionaires, porter etc.);

(iv)   guests' accident and theft;

(v)   cash (to cover what can be considerable quantities circulating in the hotel);

(vi)   loss of bar licence;

(vii)   consequential loss;

(viii)   hotel contents;

(ix)   fidelity insurance (to cover all cashiers and other employees handling cash);

(x)   plate glass.

Travel agents

Hotels often have special arrangements with travel agents, tour operators, airlines or other bodies. Bookings through these agents are often at discount rates. The guest booking through a travel agent will either pay the agent or the hotel. In the former case the hotel bills the travel agent for the relevant sum less discount. In the latter case the hotel may render a 'self invoice' to the agent for commission. The analysis of gross sales and commission may need to be considered thoroughly and the travel agent's debtors at the year end analysed to ensure provision is adequate. The auditor may wish to consider the controls in place to ensure that travel agent's invoices do actually represent guests who have arrived and paid at the hotel. There may also be disputes arising when guests decide to stay longer at the hotel than originally booked, or if they shorten their stay.

Promotions

Hotels may often run promotions by way of free hospitality and entertainment. Controls should be in place, e.g. dummy bills, to ensure the costs of this entertainment are controlled. If hospitality sales are not recorded there must be a question mark over the adequacy of internal controls being exercised or the risk of non-recording bona fide sales.

Minor operating assets

Hotels require a considerable level of furnishing and various items of crockery etc. and these will constantly require renewal. The minimum level of furnishing is generally referred to as base operating stock. This is dealt with by three main methods.

(A)   When the hotel is originally set up, all such furnishings are capitalised, subsequently all replacements are written off and additions are added to the base.

(B)   Base operating stock is capitalised in full and the amount carried forward each year is depreciated by a fixed percentage amount. Replacements are capitalised at cost and an assessment made of the written down value of what has been replaced which is then written off. Additions of assets not included in the base stock are capitalised and then depreciated.

(C)   In some hotels disposables such as crockery, cutlery, linen etc. are written off as purchased and only more substantial items such as furniture, fixtures and fittings and equipment are capitalised. These are then depreciated or simply held at base stock level.

Guests' expenses

Guests often require goods and services which have to be bought in from third parties (e.g. flowers, theatre tickets, taxis or car hire). These costs are recovered directly from the guest and the conventional treatment is to net off the related income and expenditure in the accounts except for any additional administration charge made. It is as essential that these 'pay outs' are picked up as quickly by the billing system as any others.

Payroll

5.24   Staff, within the hotel industry, are employed under a variety of payment methods. Management, reception and senior restaurant staff tend to be employed on a fixed annual salary. In contrast, bar kitchen and cleaning staff are normally paid on an hourly rate, adjusted as necessary for unsociable hours' payments. Part-time employees are common in both fixed and hourly paid occupations.

Common benefits in kind, given to staff, include free or subsidised meals, accommodation, holiday packages etc. The Inland Revenue needs to be consulted, in cases where the benefits are regarded as essential to the employees fulfilling their duties e.g. accommodation for night staff.

There are also a large proportion of temporary staff employed in the hotel trade, either employed as casuals or fixed-term employees. The payment method depends both on the expected length of employment and the type of work being undertaken. Temporary staff employed for tasks that are normally paid on the basis of an hourly rate, for example, bar and cleaning work, are likely to be paid as casuals. However, temporary reception and administration staff are usually given fixed-term contracts.

Payroll is an important area for both the audit and the internal financial control. Not only is it a major component of most hotels' costs but it is also a complex area because of the variety of employment methods used. Therefore management would be expected to spend a large proportion of their time on payroll related matters; controlling costs and ensuring all PAYE and NIC legislation is understood and followed.

Reports on small company acounts

5.25   As outlined in 5.1 above, in November 1993 the Chancellor announced the intention to abolish completely the requirement for an audit for companies with a turnover below £90,000. For companies with a turnover between £90,000 and £350,000 the Chancellor said that there would be an option to replace the audit requirement by an audit exemption report. The DTI subsequently issued further details. Companies satisfying the turnover thresholds will be automatically exempted from the statutory audit requirement provided that, in addition:

(*a*)   their gross assets do not exceed £1.4 million;

(*b*)   they are not public limited companies, part of group structure or subject to a statute-based regulatory regime, such as *Financial Services Act 1985*;

(*c*)   the exemption has not been vetoed by shareholders holding 10 per cent or more of the share capital.

The proviso of not being part of a group will mean that small wholly-owned subsidiaries will still need to have a statutory audit.

What is an audit exemption?

5.26   If a company has a turnover between £90,000 and £350,000 (or gross income of between £90,000 and £250,000 for a charitable company), it can have an audit exemption report. This report must state whether, in the opinion of the reporting accountant making it:

(*a*)   the accounts of the company are in agreement with the accounting records kept by the company under *Companies Act 1985, s 221, Pt VII, Ch I*; and

(b)   having regard only to, and on the basis of, the information contained in those accounting records, those accounts have been drawn up in a manner consistent with the accounting provisions of the *Companies Act 1985*, so far as applicable to the company; and

(c)   the audit exemption conditions have been met by the company and, at no time during the year did the company fall within a non-exempt category (e.g. public company, member of a group, banking company, etc.).

Who can give an audit exemption report?

5.27   The audit exemption report must be given by a 'reporting accountant', who must be independent of the company. The reporting accountant can be a Registered Auditor. Otherwise, a member of either the Institute of Chartered Accountants of England and Wales, Scotland or Ireland or a member of the Chartered Association of Certified Accountants or the Association of Authorised Public Accountants can be the reporting accountant. This is provided the member can engage in public practice, which for the ICAEW means holding a practising certificate and professional indemnity insurance.

Directors' responsibility

5.28   If the exemptions are taken advantage of, the directors must make a statement on the balance sheet covering the following points:

(a)   that the company was entitled to the exemption from an audit;

(b)   that no members (i.e. over 10 per cent) have requested an audit;

(c)   that the directors acknowledge their responsibilities for ensuring that the company keeps accounting records which comply with all the disclosure requirements of the *Companies Act 1985*. The accounts have still to be filed at Companies House within ten months of the year end.

Abbreviated accounts

5.29   Small-and medium-sized companies have been able to file abbreviated accounts with the registrar of companies (though full accounts must be prepared and audited for the members).

If a company which satisfies the report conditions proposes to take advantage of the exemptions conferred by *Schedule 8, Pt III* (on delivery of accounts) and deliver abbreviated accounts to the registrar of companies an exemption report must also be delivered. No specific report by the reporting accountant on the abbreviated accounts is required.

Implementation

5.30   The commencement date for the regulations is 11 August 1994. The transitional provisions mean that the audit exemption will apply to any annual accounts of a company approved by the board of directors on or after the date on which the regulations come into force. This is provided the accounts were not overdue for filing before 1 August 1994 at Companies House. The exemption from audit will apply automatically each year to companies which satisfy the criteria. If in a following year the criteria are not met, in full or in part, the company will not be exempt. There will be no transitional relief as there is for small companies and abbreviated accounts.

If the year end is before the commencement date, or less than one month after that date, shareholders owning 10 per cent or more of the shares will have one month from the commencement date to lodge a letter requiring the company to obtain an audit. If they do, the audit exemption will not apply.

Audit exemption reports – statement of standards for reporting accountants (SSRA)

5.31   The Auditing Practices Board (APB) has issued a Statement of Standards for Reporting Accountant's (SSRA) on audit exemption reports. It gives guidance on the reports for small companies that will be exempted from the statutory audit requirement, but require the services of a reporting accountant. The SSRA's requirements include the following.

(*a*)   The reporting accountant should perform such procedures as are necessary to provide a reasonable basis on which to express the opinions that are to be provided in the report.

(*b*)   The reporting accountant and the company should set out in writing, and agree on, the terms of the engagement. The conduct of the engagement should comply with the ethical guidance issued by the reporting accountant's relevant professional body.

(*c*)   The reporting accountant should plan their work so an effective engagement is performed.

(*d*)   If work is delegated to assistants, it should be directed, supervised and reviewed in a manner that provides confidence that such work will be done competently, in accordance with the statement of standards.

(*e*)   Working papers should adequately record the reporting accountant's planning, and the procedures performed, and should provide evidence that the work was carried out in accordance with these standards and support the conclusions drawn.

(*f*)   The reporting accountant should perform such procedures as are necessary to provide a reasonable basis on which to express an opinion using only the information in the accounting records on whether the company accounts have been drawn up in a manner consistent with *Companies Act 1985, s 249C(6)* and the company is entitled to exemption from an audit.

(*g*)   If the reporting accountant either doubts whether the results of the examination procedures provide a reasonable basis on which to express an affirmative opinion on each of the matters specified by the *Act*, or comes across information indicating that the accounts may be misleading, the matters giving rise to these concerns should be discussed with the directors.

(*h*)   The audit exemption report should include a title identifying the company's shareholders as the persons to whom the report is addressed, an introductory paragraph identifying the accounts examined, a statement that the directors are responsible for the preparation of the accounts, a description of the basis of the reporting accountant's opinion, the reporting accountant's opinion, the name and signature of the reporting accountant and the date of the report.

(*j*)   If the reporting accountant concludes that in respect of a particular matter the accounts either are not in agreement with those accounting records kept by the company under *section 221* or have not been drawn up in a manner consistent with the accounting requirements specified in *section 249C(4)*, the report should include a negative opinion in respect of the relevant part of the opinion section.

(*k*)   If a limitation on the scope of the examination procedures prevents the reporting accountant from obtaining a reasonable basis for an unqualified opinion, the opinion should be qualified in respect of the relevant part of the opinion section.

(*l*)   If the reporting accountants have become aware of information which indicates to them that their concerns cannot be resolved by procedures which are within the scope of the examination they should add an explanatory paragraph to the 'basis or opinion' section of the report, referring to the matter. It should be clearly stated that no opinion is expressed on the matter referred to.

Chapter 6

Income and Expenditure

Departmental activity

6.1   The activities of an hotel are frequently divided into different departments to reflect the fact that hotels provide a number of different services, each of which has different costs involved and is usually under the responsibility of a separate manager. Within an hotel the various services provided can include everything from the accommodation to sports facilities, restaurant, conference and function facilities. The services provided can be split into three main areas which are accommodation, food and beverage and 'other'. The 'other' category catches services such as functions and conference facilities or any other unusual services that an individual hotel may provide.

In order to keep effective control of costs and revenues each department is usually treated as a separate cost centre so that the management can have a clear grasp of how each department is performing. In this way accounts can be prepared which match the income and expenditure of each department. The major benefit of this is that the performance of each department can be monitored via movements of both sales and the gross margins so that both the sales performance and the control of costs can be exposed and analysed. Individual department managers can consequently be held responsible if their department is underperforming and a plan can be implemented to recover the situation. Similarly the department managers can be rewarded according to their performance. In addition, direct costs known as controllables can be monitored and controlled.

The operation is divided into departments.

Interest rates

6.2   Overheads are equally important. In recent times the overhead that has caused the most headaches has been interest charges which were unusually high in the late 1980s and early 1990s. This combined with overvalued property prices left many hotels in a position of being both too highly geared and having to finance extremely high interest bills. Clearly fluctuations in interest rates are out of the hands of an hotelier, but he can budget for the level of gearing that he considers acceptable and which the business is able to finance. He can also make use of fixed rate options and other financing packages such as collars to limit his exposure to fluctuations in the interest rate. These instruments effectively insure the business against adverse movements in base rates, but of course there are costs involved in the form of paying fixed interest rates which are higher than prevailing fluctuating rates. Other costs may include arrangement fees. Many companies are caught out because they fail to plan properly for worst case scenarios. For instance it is easy to calculate that a company can afford interest payments if rates rise to a certain point, e.g. up to 15 per cent, but the analysis should go a step further and consider what happens if that hike in interest rates coincides (as it is likely to do) with a drop of turnover. In such circumstances the pincer effect can ensure that only a marginal drop in turnover is enough to tip the company over the edge and into an insolvent position, as indeed happened with many hotel companies in the last recession. In September 1994 interest rates were raised by half a percentage point, marking the end of the downward trend in interest that had prevailed since the UK's exit from the ERM. In the current economic climate it is unlikely that interest rates will fluctuate widely in one direction or another. However, this rise illustrates how this particular overhead is beyond the immediate control of an individual business. As a result it is extremely important that plans are formulated to control the exposure of the business to these fluctuations by not overborrowing and using financial instruments to limit exposure where appropriate.

Heat and light

6.3   Another major overhead is 'heat and light'. On a medium- to long-term basis hotel management can plan to reduce their demand for these services via investment in energy saving products such as better insulation. In the short term these costs can be hard to control. There is some scope for negotiating better deals with alternative suppliers in the wake of recent moves to increase competition in the gas and electricity supply industries. Even so, changing suppliers is only likely to have a significant impact on bills if the hotel is a large user and therefore able to exert stronger bargaining power.

Accommodation

6.4   Accommodation is usually the most important service that an hotel provides, however, in terms of sales this is not always the case, especially if the hotel provides substantial other services, e.g. conference facilities. According to Horwath International in 1991 45.5 per cent of total revenues of UK provincial hotels stemmed from rooms. In London the figure rises to some 61.6 per cent.

On the revenue side the key factors for an hotel to consider are the rates it charges for its rooms against the level of occupancy it needs to achieve at each level of potential average room rate. In other words it is the same equation that any other business must consider: what price for what turnover? Clearly, pricing depends upon the market sector that the hotel is targeting, although the starting point should be to work out the break even points for the hotel at various levels of turnover and pricing.

As a general principle it is better to sacrifice a certain amount on the average room rate in order to achieve high levels of occupancy, especially since each guest is a captive market to whom the hotel can sell its other services. However, a hotel should know what its marginal costs of selling a room are in order that the hotelier is aware of the selling price below which no contribution to operating profit will be made. If the hotel is likely to have empty rooms it generally makes sense for the hotelier to offer discounts right down to that point since some contribution is better than none, and because of the guests' tendency to make use of the hotel's other services. A major reason a hotel may prefer to have empty rooms rather than make significant discounts is if it is an upmarket operation whose goodwill within its target market may suffer as a result of discounting.

A system of yield management has been developed in the USA to tackle the problem of the trade-off between room rate and occupancy and is now in widespread use in the UK. It relies upon creating a database of information on the type of trade and customers that a hotel services. A bank of information is built up which the system can then use to predict the optimum rooms rates for that hotel at a particular time of year. It can also assist the management in making decisions such as the age-old problem of whether to sell a room at a discount to a customer or wait for more customers willing to pay higher rates to arrive later on.

It is a characteristic of the accommodation side of an hotel's business that gross margins will be high reflecting the low direct costs involved in the housekeeping that is required to clean the rooms and change the sheets and so on. The real cost of accommodation lies in the capital investment that is tied up in the building and the costs of maintaining the fabric of the building as well as providing the furniture, fixtures and fittings that are necessary. Control of the housekeeping costs is usually the responsibility of the housekeeper. This involves setting standard amounts of time that it should take to clean each room to the required standard. It is then a matter of allocating a certain amount of rooms to each cleaner and monitoring the time it takes each of them to achieve their task. This is important, especially since cleaners tend to be paid on an hourly rate.

The other major direct cost of accommodation lies in the provision of clean linen. Most hotels contract this out to specialists who remove the dirty sheets and replace them with clean sets. Usually the linen is the property of the contractor. The cost to the hotel lies in the rates it pays the contractor for the services. It can keep control of these costs by ensuring an accurate record is kept of the numbers of items that the contractor takes away to clean. This can then be checked against the contractor's bills to ensure that no overcharging is taking place. Contractors also sometimes insist on minimum wash charges. This is in effect a minimum charge for the period and can be significant if the hotel experiences wide fluctuations in demand between high and low seasons. It is usually smaller hotels that suffer from this type of charge, and should be particularly careful when negotiating long-term contracts with contractors.

Food and beverage

6.5   Although food and beverage are put together under the same headings, they are usually run as separate departments, especially in larger hotels. The restaurant side of an hotel's business is usually run like any other restaurant. The one major difference is likely to be in the marketing of the restaurant since in an hotel it will be largely dependent upon the hotel guests for its clientele. On the revenue side the pricing of its meals will be determined by the type of market that the hotel itself targets. It will usually aim to pitch its prices such that the guests will prefer to eat in rather than go out and search for an alternative restaurant. This will be much affected by the proximity or otherwise of other restaurants in the vicinity of the hotel. It may also be partly determined by the extent to which the hotel wishes to attract the general public to use its restaurant.

The direct costs of a restaurant are chiefly concerned with labour costs and purchases of dry stocks (food) and wet stocks (beverages). The cost of purchases can be significantly reduced if the operation is part of a larger group with some level of central purchasing. The larger the group's spending power the larger the discounts it is likely to be able to negotiate owing to its purchasing power. On the other hand a single restaurant is unlikely to be able to negotiate such discounts since its orders will generally not be of a bulk nature. Cost of labour will depend upon the hours of opening and the number of clientele regularly served. In many cases decisions are taken to open restaurants for meals such as breakfast or lunch which, if viewed on their own would not be economic due to labour costs. But in an hotel it is often necessary for marketing purposes to provide for every meal so that a comprehensive service can be offered.

Most hotels provide some, if not all, of their staff meals while on duty. This is a further cost that the restaurant will have to cater for which can significantly dent the profitability of the restaurant department unless the costs are attributed to the other departments in accordance with the number of staff that are fed. Due to these extra burdens that are often put upon restaurants in hotels, especially where meals are catered for at a loss, the profitability of the restaurant department can be low. However, the extra goodwill and the marketing benefits to the hotel as a whole should more than make up for this. The issues involved in providing a bar service as regards pricing and cost are not dissimilar to those issues encountered in a restaurant department.

Specialist services

6.6   The other services that an hotel may provide can be numerous and each has its own specialist issues and problems. The most common 'specialist' service may be some form of conference and/or function facilities. These require roughly the same resources and skills since both require a large room in which to hold the event and both often require meals and drinks to be provided. The largest difference may arise in the marketing of these facilities since functions tend to target both corporate bodies, for instance Christmas parties, but also private individuals for events such as weddings. Conferences on the other hand are entirely the domain of corporations and other organisations such as trade unions. Any other services that are provided will usually require specialist skills beyond those that an hotelier may be expected to have. For example a sports centre must be run by someone qualified and experienced in that field.

Chapter 7

Tax Issues

Introduction

Carrying on the trade – sole trader, partnership or company

7.1   This chapter is a brief guide to some of the important tax issues involved in the hotel industry. More detailed information can be found in *Tolley's Income Tax 1995-96*, *Corporation Tax 1995-96* and *Capital Gains Tax 1995-96*.

Tax considerations on the choice of trading vehicle include the following.

(*a*)   The rates of income tax and national insurance which vary between an unincorporated trader and a company director receiving salary and/or dividends. In general, for a young growing business, it may be better for the trader to operate in an unincorporated vehicle. Once profits reach a certain level, it may then be appropriate to incorporate. A sole trader or partner pays tax at up to 40 per cent when his total taxable income for the year exceeds £24,300 (1995/96), while a company continues to pay tax at 25 per cent on profits up to £300,000.

(*b*)   The timing of tax payments differs between companies and unincorporated traders. Under the Pay and File system of tax payment for companies, a company must estimate its own tax liability and pay this to the Revenue within nine months of the end of its accounting period. Within twelve months of the end of its accounting period it must send in a detailed corporation tax return, accounts and computations.

The timing of tax payments does not depend on the date to which accounts are drawn up for an unincorporated business. Tax is due in two instalments on 1 January within the tax year and 1 July after the tax year concerned. These instalments will be based on an estimated assessment of the tax due on profits of the *preceding tax year*, and in due course a more accurate assessment of tax for the year will be issued, leading to repayments or further payments of tax for the year concerned. However, unincorporated businesses which commence after 5 April 1994 will be subject to a new regime for the taxation of income. Under the new system

107

tax will be based on the profits of the accounting period ending in the tax year under consideration, rather than of the preceding year.

From 1997/98 all businesses will be taxed in this way. The taxpayer will have the choice of preparing his own assessment of the tax due, in which case the tax payment and his return will be due by 31 January after the tax year, or of providing all the information to the Revenue for the purpose of assessing his tax, in which case the return will be due by 30 September after the tax year. Under this new regime for individuals, tax will be payable in two instalments, on 31 January within the tax year and 31 July after the tax year. These will be estimates of the current liability, based on the final tax liability for the previous year. Then on 31 January *after* the tax year, the taxpayer will pay a top-up payment to finalise the liability for the year. The new regime is designed to smooth out the payments of tax due from an individual taxpayer, but professional advice will still be needed on the completion of the return, the amounts of tax due, and the transition to the new regime (which in many cases will not be complete until 1997/98). Transitional rules will apply to the crossover year 1996/97.

(c)   The treatments of tax losses and of capital gains tax differ substantially between unincorporated businesses and companies. One of the main considerations is that a double charge to CGT may arise on running an hotel through a company, in the absence of proper tax planning, once where a property is sold and then later when the shares in the company are sold. A property held directly by the proprietor of the business would only suffer one such charge to CGT on disposal.

(d)   Pension arrangements for the proprietor of an unincorporated business differ substantially from those for a director or employee of a company.

PAYE and NIC issues

7.2   The payment of salaries to hotel staff is likely to present a number of particular PAYE and NIC issues. The hotel is likely to employ staff on a seasonal, casual or part-time basis and there may be the question of whether individuals who provide their services to the hotel are employed or self-employed (see 3.27 above). Whatever the issues relevant to a particular hotel, the Inland Revenue is likely to pay close attention to this industry, and time spent in ensuring that tax and NIC matters are correctly reported and dealt with will save a great deal of trouble in the event of a visit from one of the Revenue's PAYE audit teams.

Employed or self-employed?

7.3   In the case of most hotel staff members, it will be quite clear whether they are self-employed or employed. Room cleaners, reception staff, bar and maintenance staff are all likely to be employees and subject to PAYE tax and

NIC at source on their salaries. In most cases it would be impossible to argue that they were anything other than employees of the hotel, and in any event, they would probably be content to retain their status, in spite of the tax and NIC considerations, because of the uncertainties and responsibilities of declaring themselves self-employed.

However, other categories of workers in hotels may be clearly self-employed. This may be because the services they provide are so obviously those of an independent business person, e.g. an electrician engaged to carry out a specific contract and no more, or a tennis coach at the hotel's sports facilities who is not based in the hotel and provides his services at many other hotels without being based at any of them.

A third group of workers may claim to be self-employed after a period of employment with an hotel, either on their own initiative or that of the hotel. Or they may begin work at the hotel and claim to be self-employed from the start. The obvious attractions in being classified as self-employed that arise from the lower NIC rates, the more generous deduction of expenses and the delay in the payment of tax can lead to mistakes in categorisation that can prove expensive to resolve with the Revenue or the Contributions Agency.

A string of court cases in a number of different fields (tax, social security, employment law, liability in negligence cases) has supplied a fairly clear set of considerations in the argument over whether a person is employed or self-employed. However, the order of priority of these considerations given by the courts tends to shift over the years, just as the Revenue's chosen areas of attack tend to change. The most recent high-profile case was of *Hall v Lorimer (1994) 23 STC* concerning a technician in the broadcasting industry. It is also worth noting that one of the court cases in this area, *O'Kelly v Trusthouse Forte plc (1983) 3 WLR 605* concerned staff employed by a major London hotel.

As well as operating a normal hotel and restaurant business, the employers also carried on a business of hiring out rooms for private functions for which they provided catering services. As a result of the seasonal nature of this business, the staff were not permanent employees, but were placed on a general list of available individuals. Certain 'regulars' could be relied on to provide their services regularly, and who in return could rely on the availability of regular work. This situation was considered for employment law purposes, and the court approved the decision of an Employment Appeal Tribunal that the regulars were not employed in this capacity, but were self-employed. Although many factors were consistent with a contract of employment, such as the fact that the staff performed work under the direction and control of management, the crucial element missing was 'mutuality of obligation' – the staff were not obliged to report for work on particular occasions, and the management was not obliged to provide work.

Tips and Troncs

7.4   A 'tronc' is the term given to a system whereby gratuities or service charges in a restaurant or hotel are paid into a central collection point and then paid out by one of the staff or management to the waiters, waitresses, and bar staff (see 5.10 above) who have earned them. The person who makes the payments out (who may be known as the 'Tronc Master' is treated under PAYE law as the employer making a payment of emoluments. The Tronc Master should operate a PAYE system separate from the system being operated by the hotel or restaurant as the main employer, and it is the Tronc Master who should prepare end of year PAYE returns and complete the relevant sections of P46s or P45s when employees start or leave employment. As an alternative to deduction of tax through PAYE at the time the tips are paid, the Revenue may be prepared to include the amount of tips received by an employee in their notice of coding.

Where a tronc system is started for the first time, the main employer should get in touch with their tax office to give details of who will be the Tronc Master. If the person who would be designated as Tronc Master under the PAYE regulations does not comply with these rules, the main employer may become liable to pay the tax, with possible interest and penalty consequences.

In the case of *Figael v Fox (1992) 83 STC,* a restaurant operated a system of collecting tips which were divided at the end of each week between the directors of the company and the staff. There was no formal appointment of any person to take responsibility for the arrangements, and the directors did not keep any record of the tips they had distributed. The Revenue raised a determination under what is now *Regulation 49* of the *Income Tax (Employments) Regulations 1993 (SI 1993 No 744)* to collect tax from the company, but the company argued that the arrangements in fact fell within what is now *Regulation 5*, i.e. that the directors had been acting as Tronc Masters and should have operated PAYE. However, the Commissioners decided on these facts that it was the company that had made the division of tips and not the directors or anyone else acting as Tronc Master. The High Court and the Court of Appeal affirmed this decision.

Where a tronc system as envisaged by *Regulation 5* is not operated, but customers and guests pay tips direct to staff without ever passing through the till or through management, there is no obligation for the hotel or restaurant to account to the Revenue for the sums involved. However, the member of staff should include the amounts of tips on his own personal tax return, even though his contract may make no mention of the way in which tips should be treated.

Many tips in hotels and restaurants are now paid by the customer entering a figure on their credit card statement for an amount to be paid to the member of staff, perhaps in addition to a service charge. The Revenue apparently takes the view that such amounts should be subject to PAYE as described above in any case where the employer pays out the cash amount of this discretionary payment to the member of staff. The only case in which PAYE need not be operated is where members of staff settle up with a till or master till at the end of their shift, up to an amount that is calculated as due by the till, by handing over cheques, credit card slips and cash, so that they retain an amount which has been collected by them but is not due to the till, i.e. the amounts they have been given in tips.

On the NIC side, tips or other gratuities paid to staff are entirely excluded from earnings liable to NICs provided the payment is not made either directly or indirectly by the employer and is not allocated by the employer to the earner. Tips are therefore excluded from NIC liability where tips are paid directly to the member of staff by the guest or customer, or paid into a staff box or to someone who is acting independently of the employer. For NIC purposes, tips can be paid to and distributed by a Tronc Master or 'tronc committee' without a liability arising, provided such a person or persons are acting independently of the main employer. This position is thus different from the income tax treatment described above.

Service charges

7.5   The DSS's view is that *service charges* (as opposed to tips) which are collected by the employer and distributed to employees are earnings for NIC purposes, as these are not voluntary payments which the payer is not obliged to make, and they do pass indirectly through the employer.

Casual and temporary staff, agency workers and students

7.6   Hotels and their restaurants may engage short-term staff of one kind or another and should take care to operate PAYE procedures correctly. For new casual and temporary staff, the employer should follow Cards 4 and 5 of the employer's guide to PAYE (P8).

ICTA 1988, s 134 applies to workers supplied via an agency. Subject to certain exemptions and restrictions, any payment made by either the agency or the client of the agency, that is the hotelier in this case, is deemed to be an emolument subject to PAYE. In the majority of cases, the hotelier will pay the agency in return for supplying the worker's services, and the agency will pay the employee so that the PAYE obligation will be on the agency. In other cases, the hotelier will pay a commission to the agency and will pay remuneration to the worker, in which case the hotelier must include the worker on his PAYE paperwork and deduct tax from remuneration paid.

Students may take employment with hotels during their longer vacations, and the normal rules applicable to new employees would need to be followed if they were expected to earn above the PAYE threshold. If the student thinks that his total taxable income in the year is likely to be less than his personal allowance, he can fill in Form 38(S) and give it to the employer, who then does not need to deduct tax. Any tax that has already been deducted before Form 38 (S) has been completed can be repaid to the student. This does not apply to students who do evening or part-time work outside normal education holiday times, or to students who work both during *and* outside holiday times.

Accommodation and other services provided to staff

7.7   Where staff are provided with living accommodation, whether long-term or temporary, this provision is likely to be treated as a taxable emolument of that member of staff. The employee will be taxed on the value of the accommodation to him for any period, less any sum made good by him to the management of the hotel. [*ICTA 1988, s 145*]. The value of the accommodation is given by the gross rateable value of the accommodation or any actual rent, if greater, paid by the owner of the hotel in respect of the accommodation. As the latter measure of value is unlikely to be relevant, the value taken will be the gross rateable value. This measure is obviously one that was relevant under the general rating system that operated for local government financing before 1 April 1990 in England and Wales, but has since been replaced first by the community charge and then (from 1 April 1993 in England and Wales) by the council tax. In view of these changes the Government is currently reviewing this measure of the value of the benefit of accommodation. Meanwhile, the last available gross rateable value of property, under the old domestic rating lists, will continue to give the value of such accommodation for tax purposes. For new properties, and those where there has been a considerable change of circumstances (e.g. change of use), employers themselves will be asked to provide an estimate of what the gross rateable value would have been had the old rating system continued. In practice, the value of the benefit of accommodation is likely to be arrived at by negotiation with the inspector of taxes. On the employee's P11D, the employer should provide all details of living or other accommodation provided to employees or directors.

The above charge to tax does not apply where:

(*a*)   it is necessary for the proper performance of his duties for the employee to reside in the accommodation;

(*b*)   the employment is such that it is customary for employees to be provided with accommodation for the better performance of their duties; or

(*c*)   the employer is an individual and the provision of accommodation is made in the normal course of his domestic, family or personal relationships [*ICTA 1988, s 145(4)(7)*];

(*d*)   there is a special threat to this security, special security arrangements are in force and he resides in the accommodation as part of those arrangements.

In the context of hotels, there will be a number of categories of staff to whom this tax charge may not apply, for instance night staff and security staff. In some cases, the inspector may argue for a charge under *section 145* on the grounds that it is not customary for such a member of staff to be provided with accommodation, and it will be necessary to compare the situation in question with hotels of a similar standard and location to answer this point. Although a charge under *section 145* may not apply where the accommodation is made to family or friends, the other side to this is that expenses associated with the accommodation provided will not be deductible as trading expenses (see *ICTA 1988, s 74 (a)(b)*).

On the NIC side, where an employer provides free board and lodgings for an employee, neither the costs nor the value of these lodgings are included in the employee's gross pay for NIC purposes (NI 269). On the other hand any reimbursement of board and lodging costs will only be so excluded if it is a reimbursement of expenses actually incurred by the employee in carrying out his employment.

Interest relief

7.8   Whether an hotelier needs to take out a loan to purchase a property for use as an hotel or to finance an extension or improvement of the hotel, one major consideration will be the availability of tax relief on the interest paid on the loan. If the hotelier is not trading through a company, but as a sole trader or in partnership, relief for interest paid will generally be available as a trading expense. Except in the case of interest paid abroad, interest may qualify as a trading expense if it is incurred on revenue account and is wholly and exclusively incurred for the purposes of the trade. Relief is available for interest on bank overdrafts and other temporary facilities as well as on longer-term loans secured by the assets of the business.

Where a loan is taken out partly for the purpose of the hotel business and partly for some other purpose, it may be possible to make an apportionment of the interest so that relief is available for part of the interest paid. This will depend on agreement with the inspector of taxes that such an apportionment is appropriate in a particular case.

Where interest is paid abroad, it and the loan must satisfy further conditions. Relief will not be available to the extent that interest is paid at more than a commercial rate. [*ICTA 1988, s 74 (n)*]. *Yearly* interest paid to a non-resident must also satisfy one of the conditions in *ICTA 1988, s 82*. Yearly interest is essentially interest on a loan that is capable of being repayable after more than one year. The conditions in *section 82* are fairly complex, but essentially can be satisfied where the payer of the interest who is carrying on the trade is a resident of the UK and the interest is payable in a currency other than sterling. Because of the conditions attached to the payment of interest abroad, an hotelier would generally be best advised to borrow from a UK lender.

Where the trade of hotel management is run by a partnership, interest relief can be obtained either on loans taken out by the partnership itself or by individual partners. Under *ICTA 1988, s 362*, an individual member of a partnership may receive a deduction from his income of money contributed to the partnership as capital, where the money is used wholly for the purposes of the partnership trade. The *Finance Act 1994* brought some amelioration in the method of relief given for interest on loans to partnerships and certain other loans. Prior to the *Finance Act 1994*, the interest had to be 'annual interest' chargeable on receipt to Schedule D Case III, and had to be interest payable in the UK on a loan from a bank carrying on business in the UK or Eire or the stockmarket. [*ICTA 1988, s 353 (1)*]. The *Finance Act 1994* amended this general provision so that relief is now available for any interest that satisfies the conditions of *section 362* or the related provisions. This will be of particular use to non-UK resident borrowers whose interest payments may not have a UK source and who previously would not have been able to satisfy the qualifying conditions.

Hoteliers who carry on their trade through a company may obtain interest relief either as a deduction from trading profits (where the loan is taken out wholly and exclusively for the purposes of the trade and the interest is paid to a bank carrying on business in the UK) or as a charge on income in other circumstances. Where interest is not paid to a bank carrying on business in the UK, it should generally be paid over net of basic rate tax, which should be accounted for to the Inland Revenue.

Capital allowances

7.9   Capital expenditure on the construction or purchase of hotel buildings can be written down against taxable income in two ways. These are:

(*a*)   if the hotel is a 'qualifying hotel' outside an enterprise zone; and

(*b*)   if the hotel is sited in an enterprise zone.

Enterprise zones are areas designated by the Government for various special allowances, including favourable capital allowances. About forty enterprise zones have been designated, and each zone has a ten-year life during which expenditure can qualify for allowances, although in some cases allowances are available after the expiry of this time.

Qualifying hotels

7.10   Hotels outside the enterprise zones can only qualify for capital allowances if they are 'qualifying hotels'. This means that the hotel:

(*a*)   must have its accommodation in a building of a permanent nature;

(*b*)   must be open for at least four months in the season (the season being defined as April to October inclusive);

(*c*) must have at least ten private bedrooms available for letting to the public, and the sleeping accommodation must consist wholly or mainly of rooms which are not normally in occupation for more than a month; *and*

(*d*) must provide services including the provision of breakfasts and an evening meal, the making of beds and the cleaning of rooms. (This last rule is regarded as satisfied even where breakfast or an evening meal is available only on request.)

Where a qualifying hotel is carried on by an individual alone, or in partnership, any accommodation that is used as a dwelling by him or by a member of his family when the hotel is open, is not regarded as part of the hotel, and so capital allowances will not be available on that portion of the expenditure.

Allowances are available on qualifying expenditure on qualifying hotels. The definition of qualifying expenditure is broadly the same as for that on industrial buildings, that is it excludes expenditure on the acquisition of land, but includes the cost of preparation work on the site of the building, such as preparing, cutting, or levelling land, and the cost of laying foundations. Fees of architects, surveyors and other professionals may be included in the qualifying expenditure where they are integral to it.

Qualifying expenditure on a qualifying hotel is written down against taxable profits at the rate of 4 per cent a year on the straight-line basis. In a simple case, therefore, the qualifying capital expenditure is relieved completely against profits after 25 years, or on the building ceasing to be used as an hotel, a 'balancing adjustment' will arise. This will be either an allowance of the residual amount of qualifying expenditure, or a taxable charge in cases where the building is sold for more than this residual amount. Where the hotel is transferred to a person who is connected to the owner, they can elect that no 'balancing adjustment' occurs, so that the new owner carries on receiving the writing-down allowances of the old owner, until the 25-year life has expired.

Example

The Tower Hotel Partnership buys land for £2 million and spends £5 million constructing a qualifying hotel. The hotel is built and brought into use in the tax year 1989/90. In 1999/2000 it is sold to another hotel chain for £2.5 million.

In 1989/90 and for each year until 1998/99 (nine years altogether), a writing-down allowance is available against taxable profits of:

4% x £5 million = £200,000

E.g. in 1999/2000 £1,800,000 has been written down, leaving £3,200,000 of qualifying expenditure. In 1999/2000 a balancing allowance is given of:

£3,200,000 – £2,500,000 = £700,000

Hotels in enterprise zones

7.11 Hotels in enterprise zones can qualify for an *initial* allowance of 100 per cent, instead of the 4 per cent writing-down allowance described above. This is available for two types of hotels:

(*a*) those that would be 'qualifying hotels' even if located outside an enterprise zone; and

(*b*) those that would not qualify under that definition, but are in fact buildings used in the hotel trade.

In effect, this means that there are no restrictions on the number of rooms, length of season etc. for hotels to receive capital allowances in enterprise zones, provided that a substantial commercial activity is being carried on. As a 100 per cent initial allowance might exceed the taxable profit of the business in the first year or years of the business, it is possible to claim a lower amount of initial allowance. If this is done, writing-down allowances of 25 per cent are given in the following periods until the expenditure is exhausted.

Capital allowances on plant and machinery

7.12 Capital allowances are also available on expenditure on certain plant and machinery used in the hotel trade, but not if the items have been included in the qualifying expenditure on the hotel building itself. There are complex rules on what qualifies as expenditure on plant and machinery in a particular business, and on the dividing line between plant and machinery and the building itself. These rules will have a significant impact on the rate of allowance available.

In the case of an hotel, bar or restaurant, items such as specialist lighting, paintings and other decor might qualify for capital allowances on plant and machinery, where they contribute commercially towards the particular atmosphere the business is trying to create. A writing-down allowance of 25 per cent is available on qualifying expenditure.

Capital gains matters

7.13 In the normal course of events, an ongoing hotel trade is unlikely to give rise to many disposals of assets that will be chargeable to capital gains tax.

Disposals of tangible moveable property, such as plant and machinery used in the course of the hotel trade, are exempt in any case from CGT where the amount of the sales proceeds received on the disposal does not exceed £6,000. Where the amount of the sales proceeds does exceed £6,000, the chargeable gain is limited by a formula to five-thirds of the amount by which the gross proceeds exceeds £6,000, where this is less than the gain computed on the normal basis. [*TCGA 1992, s 262*].

The main charge to CGT is likely to arise on the disposal of the hotel. This may be a disposal of the freehold site of the building, or the lease of the building. It may include the disposal of the business being carried on at the hotel, or may be a disposal of the assets of the business once the business has ceased. It may be a disposal of a sole trader's or partnership's interest in the business, or of shares in the company that has been running the hotel. Very different CGT considerations will apply depending on which of these factors are relevant. Whichever of these factors do apply, it must be stressed that such a disposal usually requires considerable planning to ensure that the CGT charge on the disposal of a hotel is mitigated as far as possible.

Various forms of relief could be available on the disposal of an hotel's assets or business. The following is a summary of the available reliefs.

Rollover relief for business assets

7.14 Rollover relief is strictly a tax deferment rather than a relief. It is available to individuals and companies where the claimant receives consideration for the disposal of assets that were used and used only for the trade throughout their ownership, and the consideration is applied to the acquisition of new assets. The new assets must themselves be taken into use on acquisition, and must be used only for the purposes of the trade.

Where full rollover relief is given on an asset, the broad effect is that the consideration for, and hence the gain on disposal, of the old asset is reduced up to the amount of the proceeds reinvested in the new asset. The amount of this reduction is then deducted from the CGT cost of the new asset, with the effect that the amount of the relief given will be taxed on a later disposal of the new asset, unless the new asset is a wasting asset or will become one within 10 years. A wasting asset is an asset with a predictable life not exceeding 50 years. In such cases the gain on the old asset is held over for 10 years or until the new asset is disposed of or ceases to be used for the trade, whichever is earlier. Subsequent rollover into a non-wasting asset will affect the CGT disposal.

Rollover relief is suitable for an ongoing hotel business that disposes of assets and purchases new ones for the same trade, or in cases of successive or concurrent trades, e.g. where:

(a)   an 'old' asset was used for trade A, and a new asset will be used for trade B which was carried on successively with trade A;

(b)   the old asset was used for trade A, and a new asset will be used for a new trade B which will be commenced immediately after the disposal of the old asset; or

(c)   the old asset was used for trade A, and the new asset will be used for trade B which begins within three years of the cessation of trade A, provided the new asset was not used for any other purpose meanwhile.

The trades do not have to be the same trade, so that in these cases trade A or trade B may both be hotel trades, or one may be an hotel trade and the other not.

Rollover relief applies to land and buildings, among other classes of assets. It can apply to extensions of buildings and to capital improvements to buildings, and also to the enhancement of interests in buildings, such as where the lessee of an hotel acquires the freehold of the hotel.

There can be a problem where the assets are owned as tenants in common. The case of *Tod v Mudd (1987) 141 STC* concerned an individual who sold a business and bought an hotel out of the proceeds he received with his wife, owning it as a tenant in common (with the husband having a 75 per cent share and the wife 25 per cent). The husband provided 75 per cent of funds for the new hotel, and he and his wife were to occupy 25 per cent of the hotel building privately. The husband claimed rollover relief on the 100 per cent of the proceeds which he invested into the new venture. However, his claim for rollover relief on the business he had disposed of was restricted to 75 per cent of the proceeds he reinvested, as the taxpayer and his wife, as tenants in common were interested in every part of the property, including the non-business element.

Retirement relief

7.15   Unlike rollover relief, retirement relief is a real exemption from tax on the disposal of a share in a business or of business assets. If retirement relief follows rollover relief in respect of the same asset, the rolled-over gain can be exempted completely. Retirement relief is given only to an individual but it may be in respect of the disposal by him of his interest in an unincorporated business or of shares in a 'personal company'. A personal company is one in which the claimant owns at least 5 per cent of the shares. The claimant must have reached age 55 (unless it is ill health that is causing him to withdraw from the business). In the case of an unincorporated business, the trader must have owned the business throughout the 12 months ending with the disposal. In the case of a disposal of shares in a company, the individual must have been a full-time officer or employee of the company (including a director), who has devoted substantially the whole of his time to the company in a managerial capacity. Full retirement relief is available on gains per individual up to £250,000 and up to 50 per cent of further gains of £750,000. However, these amounts are restricted where the business or shares were not owned for the 10 years prior to the disposal. Retirement relief is potentially the most valuable CGT relief available, but the many conditions that must be met if full relief is to be given mean that the hotel owner/manager must give thought to planning for the relief well in advance of any disposal of the business.

Gifts relief

7.16   The owner of an hotel business may, for one reason or another, want to give assets used in the business (such as the hotel building) or shares in the company owning the hotel business, to an individual or a trust.

Such a gift, if made to a person who is connected with the donor, would in many cases give rise to a CGT charge as it would represent a disposal of the asset for consideration equal to the market value of the asset.

However, CGT gifts relief can be available in these circumstances, to reduce what may be a chargeable gain without any actual proceeds. Where the asset is one used for the purpose of a trade carried on by the transferor or his personal company (see 7.15 above), or where the asset is shares of the company owning the hotel business, the transferor and the person to whom the gift is made can make a joint election for gifts holdover relief. The effect of this election is similar to that for rollover relief, that is, where relief is available in full, the transferor's gain can be reduced to nil and the person who receives the gifted asset will have their liability on a future disposal of the asset increased by the amount of the relief given to the transferor.

Miscellaneous

7.17   *TMA 1970, s 14* requires the owner of a dwelling-house to make a return of all 'lodgers or inmates' resident in it, on the serving of a notice on him by an inspector of taxes. It is assumed that 'dwelling-house' includes an hotel in the ordinary sense. If any such lodger or inmate is ordinarily resident in some other place and would prefer to be assessed in that other place rather than at the dwelling-house or hotel, the owner of the dwelling-house is obliged to note the name of those individuals and the addresses at which they are ordinarily resident and would prefer to be assessed. This very old provision is not one that hoteliers will encounter very often, but it does give rise to a legal obligation. The form is not issued annually by inspectors, nor is it issued at random, but it may be issued periodically to an hotel or dwelling-house where long-term lodgers are known to stay, or as a result of 'information received' from third parties.

Chapter 8

Business Rates

Introduction

8.1   The majority of hoteliers have experienced quite dramatic increases in their rate liabilities since 1 April 1990. This date saw the introduction of the uniform business rate coupled with a rating revaluation, the first for 17 years. Now, 5 years on, the Government has revalued again. Although the Government's transitional relief system has helped soften the impact, increases in rate liabilities during a time of recession have been particularly unwelcome, especially for those hardest hit in the hotel sector.

Rating valuation

8.2   The rateable value of a property is broadly its rental value at a fixed valuation date (1 April 1988 for the 1990 Rating List and 1 April 1993 for the 1995 Rating List). The rating valuation of hotels differs from the vast majority of commercial premises which are normally valued by considering rental agreements at the fixed valuation date. Generally, as the majority of hotels are owner-occupied, rental evidence is scarce. As a consequence, recourse is given to the hotel's accounts to derive the hypothetical rent/rateable value.

A valuation based on the trading pattern of the individual hotel is a complex and technical affair. It requires knowledge of both the individual hotel and the industry generally to ensure that the resultant value is typical of the average hotel and not distorted due to some special factors attributable to the actual proprietor.

Valuations are also carried out by direct reference to the few open market rents that exist and these may be broken back to a price per equivalent double bedroom.

As a cross check the rateable value can be compared with the adjusted turnover. Historically, assessments equated to approximately 6 to 9 per cent of the adjusted turnover, with the exception of London hotels where the percentage of adjusted turnover may be higher, perhaps between 9 to 15 per cent.

The most appropriate turnover figure for rating purposes is derived from the yearly accounts just prior to the valuation date.

In some instances, no adjustment to this turnover figure is required. However, adjustments are necessary in such instances as:

(*a*) the effect of new competition in the locality since the valuation date;

(*b*) if the hotel is inefficiently managed and the turnover is not being optimised;

(*c*) high maintenance costs in comparison to more modern counterparts;

(*d*) a low profitability to turnover ratio; and

(*e*) specialist operators.

In negotiations with the Valuation Officer consideration is given to the location and age of the hotel. For example, a modern hotel in the Midlands on a major highway will be valued at a higher percentage than a family-run, Edwardian hotel in deepest Kent, where the percentage of turnover will be somewhere nearer 6 per cent.

1995 rating revaluation

8.3   The Government has committed itself to periodic property revaluations which are to be at an interval of every five years. The new revaluation came into effect from 1 April 1995. From this date every rate payer has the opportunity to appeal.

Unfortunately, the Valuation Office Agency has a vast number of appeals to deal with, and it takes time for an appeal to be settled. The usual procedure is for the appeal to be listed for hearing before a local Valuation Tribunal which initiates negotiations with the Valuation Officer. If an appropriate settlement cannot be reached, the parties present their cases before the Valuation Tribunal who in turn determine the rateable value. If either party disputes the Tribunal decision, there is a further opportunity to appeal to the Lands Tribunal. In reality, the vast majority of cases are settled by negotiation rather than Tribunal decision.

During the 1990 revaluation period, hoteliers who had exercised their right to appeal were generally justly rewarded. Negotiations with the Valuation Officer resulted, in some cases, in considerable reductions in the rating assessment.

Until negotiations commence in earnest it is too early to predict whether similar reductions will be available for the new revaluation period. Although we are generally optimistic that reductions will be forthcoming, each hotel assessment must be individually considered, and professional advice should be sought before any appeals are served. The opportunity to minimise rate liabilities should certainly not be missed. The revaluation reference date is 1 April 1993 when the industry was still reeling from the worst recession within memory and values of hotels were severely depressed.

Transitional business rate relief

8.4   The pattern of valuation changes following the 1995 revaluation varied dramatically across the country and some rate payers have benefited whilst others have lost out.

In order to try to phase in the more significant changes that have arisen, the Government has introduced transitional arrangements. These are far more restrictive than originally anticipated, proving extremely good news for those facing increases but bad news for those expecting to benefit from reductions in rate bills. The maximum increase and decrease is shown below.

New rateable value £	Annual real maximum increase 1995/6	Annual real maximum decrease 1995/6
Up to £10,000 (£15,000 in London)	7.5%	10%
Over £10,000 (£15,000 in London)	10%	5%

When inflation is reflected in the figures, this means that for 'large' properties, the actual reduction in the 1995/96 rate year is limited to a maximum of only 2.9 per cent on last year's rates bill. At the other end of the spectrum, increases can go no higher than 12.4 per cent of last year's bill.

Although the Government has proposed that the decreases in liability for the next five years will gradually rise to a maximum of 30 per cent per annum for the 1999/2000 rate year, there is further hope for those severely affected by this system. The Government has been known to change tack in the past, dispensing with downward phasing in 1993, three years into the last five-year revaluation period. This could happen again.

There are likely to be instances where, due to the effects of transitional relief, even significant reductions in assessment will result in no rate savings. In such cases no appeals should be served before the financial viability is considered by your professional adviser.

Chapter 9

VAT

Standard rate supplies in hotels

9.1 For the purposes of this section of the book, it is assumed that the reader is familiar with the basic principles of VAT, and that guidance is required specifically in relation to the hotel trade rather than capital transactions involving the sale of hotel or holiday let property.

Most sources of income received by hotel businesses will be standard rated. *VATA 1994, 9 Sch, Group 1 Item 1(d)* standard rates 'the provision in a hotel, inn, boarding house or similar establishment of sleeping accommodation or of accommodation in rooms which are provided in conjunction with sleeping accommodation or for the purpose of a supply of catering'. The term similar establishment is further defined at *Note 9* to *Group 1* as including 'premises in which there is provided furnished sleeping accommodation, whether with or without the provision of board or facilities for the preparation of food, which are used by or held out as being suitable for use by visitors or travellers'.

Hotels will also make many other sundry supplies i.e. the hotel bar, restaurant, telephone calls, dry cleaning service, sports facilities, TV and video. These all represent supplies for which payment is received and which will bear VAT at the standard rate. The tax point for VAT accounting purposes will generally be on the earlier of receipt of payment or issue of invoice. Therefore, in practical terms, this means either when cash is paid i.e. for a drink from the bar, or when an invoice is rendered at the end of the guest's stay.

Other types of accommodation

9.2 These rules apply equally to motels, guest houses, clubs providing overnight accommodation and hostels. The charge for service flats, suitable for visitors for whom the accommodation is not a permanent place of residence, will also be standard rated. However, the provision of student accommodation may be exempt under *VATA 1994, 9 Sch, Group 6*.

Holiday accommodation is also standard rated in accordance with *VATA 1994, 9 Sch, Group 1 Item 1(e)* except for certain off-season letting. Holiday accommodation is further defined by *Note 13* as including 'any accommodation in a building, hut (including a beach hut or chalet), caravan, houseboat or tent which is advertised or held out as holiday accommodation or as suitable for holiday or leisure use', but excluding any accommodation as defined at *Note 9* (see 9.1 above). Houseboats are also included in standard rating, being defined as 'boats or other floating decked structures designed or adapted for use solely as places of permanent habitation and not having means of, or capable of being readily adapted for, self propulsion'. [*VATA 1994, 8 Sch, Group 9 Item 2*].

Room only

9.3   Other supplies of rooms *only* i.e. a conference room or shop within the hotel, are exempt subject to the right to opt to tax the supply. Where, however, both accommodation and catering are supplied by the same person i.e. the hotel providing rooms and catering for a wedding reception, or private party, this is a standard rate supply.

Supplies to employees

9.4   Where employees are supplied with accommodation, food and drink and they pay for the supplies in either cash or as a deduction from salary, such amounts are deemed to be VAT inclusive. However, if these supplies are part of the employee's contractual rights there is no need to account for VAT if a deduction from wages is provided for in the contract of employment. These arrangements should, however, be agreed with Customs & Excise. Where no payment is made by the employee no VAT is due.

Tips freely given are outside the scope of VAT.

Deposits

9.5   In relation to deposits received, it is reasonably clear as a result of Tribunal decisions that deposits generally represent consideration for a supply of reserving accommodation being advance payment of the final bill, and as such VAT should be accounted for on receipt (*Customs & Excise v Moonraker's Guest House [1992] STC 544* and *Customs & Excise v Bass plc [1993] STC 42*). If a booking is cancelled and the deposit is forfeited, the hotel can reclaim any VAT already accounted for. No VAT is due on cancellation charges made, but a charge for providing any guarantee or insurance against a customer having to pay cancellation charges, is standard rated.

Long-term residents

9.6   Where there are long-term residents i.e. 29 days or more, there is a reduced VAT liability whereby VAT is only due on the value of any services provided, as the sleeping accommodation is no longer taxable. The 28-day period is not broken if a long-term guest goes away for a weekend, although where there are breaks in long-term stays, it would be wise to agree the position with Customs & Excise.

The calculation of the taxable element is the aggregate of the following:

(*a*)   cost of meals and identifiable services;

(*b*)   a minimum 20 per cent of the value of the accommodation (this being a notional value attributed to facilities provided).

Chapter 10

Obtaining Finance

Main influences

10.1   In many respects the issues involved in raising finance are the same regardless of the industry involved. Banks will always be looking for security, equity investors will demand a significant slice of scarce equity and government grants are either hard to come by or come with strings attached. However, hotels are unusual because they are both a business proposition and a property deal. There are advantages such as the security that can be offered to banks in the form of fixed charges over freeholds or leases. Hotel properties can also provide a reasonably certain estimate as to the break up value of an hotel company since they will usually have alternative uses which can be readily valued. There are also disadvantages in that property is expensive and therefore an hotel business is likely to require more capital investment than many other businesses of similar turnover, although higher margins should compensate for this.

Historical problems

10.2   During the last recession the disadvantages of being over-geared were highlighted by the large numbers of hotel companies that failed. Most of these casualties were victims of a combination of high interest rates and stagnating or declining levels of business. The high interest rates were particularly painful for hotels because of the lending spree of the mid-1980s which enabled many companies to acquire hotels at overvalued prices and at levels of gearing that in more normal times would not be considered by lenders. The resulting increase in interest costs was not sustainable in the recessionary years for many companies and the collapse in property values ensured that the shake-up of the industry has affected a large proportion of hotels in the UK. BZW estimated that up to 5 per cent of the UK hotel stock was in the hands of receivers or liquidators at the height of the recession, although it should be noted that most of these were at the smaller end of the market, particularly guest houses, bed and breakfasts and inns.

Fundamental points

10.3   The events of recent years have served to remind those involved in the hotel market that hotels are like any other business in that if investors lose sight of the basic facts of business life then they will lose money. The important basic principles revolve around supply and demand and income and expenditure. In the hotel industry it is perhaps easier to lose sight of fundamentals, for instance by viewing a transaction too much in terms of the underlying property and not giving sufficient thought to the cashflows to be generated by the business of running an hotel.

The process of raising finance in the hotel industry should be approached chiefly from the perspective of the business with the costs of financing the fixed capital of the business, the property, to be accounted and planned for in the same way that a manufacturer may plan for the costs of maintaining his plant and machinery. Within this plan therefore, contingency should be made for the worst case scenario of high interest rates which serve to increase the expense of financing the fixed capital. The value of the property from the financing point of view comes in its ability to act as security for lenders both in the form of charges and in its break-up value. Seen in this light the property is no different from the manufacturer's plant and machinery since this too can act as security and usually has a reasonably solid break-up value.

In this way an investor should look at an hotel in terms of the flows of revenue that each bedroom is capable of producing, not in terms of more traditional property formulae. The property itself is a fixed asset that must be financed like any other asset and the interest cost treated like any other overhead.

Sources and types of finance

10.4   There is a variety of sources and types of finance available, and these are discussed briefly below. Broadly speaking, these can be split into commercial and other.

Commercial

10.5   The commercial sector covers a range of sources of finance from individuals to banks to the stock market. The type of source that a business is likely to approach for finance will depend on the size of the business and the amount of finance required. A large company that is quoted on the Stock Exchange can raise funds from a wide range of sources, including from shareholders via rights issues. This chapter, however, will concentrate on the smaller unquoted company, which will not typically have this range of options available.

Equity

Equity investors are the owners of a business, whose share of the company is usually determined by the percentage of the issued shares that they own.

10.5 *Obtaining Finance*

Technically equity shareholders share between themselves the ownership of, and the rights to, the capital invested by them and the reserves after tax that have been accumulated over the history of the company. It is risk capital, meaning that should the company fail, shareholders are the last to get their money back. However, on the upside equity investors receive all the benefit of accumulated profit with no ceiling in place should the company do extremely well.

Sources of equity investment chiefly comprise the founders, directors, private investors, venture capitalists and the Stock Market. Banks are sometimes also sources of equity finance, especially in rescue situations. The type of source a company wishes to tap usually depends on size. Smaller companies tend to be most reliant upon investment by private individuals, including management and founders. Further up the scale, development capital and venture capital become increasingly important sources. The larger companies tend to be either quoted in their own right on the Stock Exchange or are a subsidiary of a parent company that is quoted.

Share capital comes in two basic varieties which are ordinary share capital and preference capital. Ordinary share capital is much as described above. Its characteristic is the right to participate with no ceiling in the profits via dividends payments. There is no guaranteed rate of return, the principle being that dividends are paid out of realised earnings and are therefore not paid when there are no accumulated earnings available. They also come last in the queue of creditors should the company be liquidated. Ordinary share capital is sometimes further divided into other categories such as 'A' Ordinary and 'B' Ordinary. This is usually done when the founders wish to ensure that they retain control of the company without necessarily owning a majority of the share capital. Examples of this can be seen in the structure of the Savoy Hotel Group and until recently in Whitbread.

Preference share capital carries the right to a fixed dividend payable out of earned profits. Preference shares rank prior to ordinary share capital for both payment of dividends and repayment of capital upon a winding up. Like ordinary share capital preference shares have a number of variations such as cumulative preference shares which entitle the holder to have any dividend arrears rolled forward until the company has accumulated sufficient profits to meet the arrears. Preference share capital was a popular means of raising capital in low inflationary areas since the capital held its real value and base rates tended not to vary dramatically. Since the 1970s, preference share capital has therefore lost some of its appeal, but is still quite common, especially in transactions involving venture capital finance.

In the hotel sector the source of equity largely depends on the size of the organisation. At the lower end of the scale the most common source of equity is the proprietor himself and his close family and friends. The larger organisations will tend to be quoted, with most of their share capital in the hands of the institutional investors.

Venture capital

In cases where a company needs further finance to expand, but is too small to become quoted and also when there is insufficient security available against which to secure a long-term bank loan then the venture capital market is often the best source for the finance required. This market specialises in high risk/ high return lending and usually invests a mixture of loans and equity into a venture. Normally venture capitalists invest in private companies and their aim is to achieve their major return on their investment from capital gains realised on exit, typically via flotation, trade sale or re-leveraging. Such finance can be advantageous to small companies aiming to achieve growth because the venture capitalist can be expected to share the financial aims of the existing owners, and to take an appropriately long-term view. It is also often the only source of finance available for such small companies looking for growth. The drawback from the company's point of view is that the venture capitalists usually demand close communications with the board, and often insist on the right to appoint a director to represent their interests. Initially they will require a great deal more information than a bank which involves more preparation. Typically they will need a comprehensive business plan (see 10.8 below). They also demand a high return with rates of around 30 to 40 per cent compounded per annum the norm. This will often involve significant dilution by the original equity investors.

The equity gap

There has been much debate in the press about the so-called equity gap. It covers companies which are too small to interest venture capitalists, but which are too big for their proprietors to be able to provide the necessary equity finance. Insofar as the equity gap can be said to exist, it is commonly suggested that it applies to companies attempting to raise equity finance in the order of £50,000 to £1,000,000.

For such companies the main options are to seek finance from banks in cases where the necessary security and/or personal guarantees are available to satisfy the banks' security cover requirements. Another possibility is to approach wealthy private individuals who wish to make a substantial investment in a small company and who will usually demand some element of control in return. Such investors have become known as 'Business Angels' and there are now various organisations and specialists who attempt to bring the two together. An example is the Venture Capital Report ('VCR'), a magazine published monthly that includes in each issue a number of investment opportunities. According to James Mallinson of VCR this source of finance is one that has been used by hotels in the past. VCR itself has found Business Angel backers for a number of hotels including the Hafton House Country Club in Scotland and Flanesford Priory in Herefordshire. It is likely that in the future this type of private investor will continue to be an important source of equity finance for the smaller organisations in the industry.

Finally, the Government has recognised this gap in the funding market and the DTI now operates a scheme whereby the DTI guarantees a significant proportion of a bank loan to a company thereby relieving the company of the requirement to provide security or personal guarantees.

Borrowing

Borrowing is a major source of finance and comes in a variety of forms from all kinds of sources. The types range from debentures issued to the public via the Stock Exchange to lease finance. It varies from equity in that the yield is in the form of interest which is offset against profit and therefore must be paid before shareholders have the right to a dividend payment. Upon a winding up it ranks before equity and frequently the lender will require further security over the business assets. Lenders have no managerial control or voting rights. As a general rule borrowing tends to be matched against the useful life of the asset or activity for which the funding is required and can be further classified as short-, medium- and long-term.

Bank borrowing

Bank borrowing is commonly used as a source of short- and medium-term finance, especially in the case of hotels where security provided by the underlying property is available. Most bank borrowing is structured either as overdraft facilities or term loans with fixed term repayment schedules.

The benefit of an overdraft lies in its flexibility. The customer only pays interest on the outstanding balance and is able to repay the loan at any time. Due to its flexibility, overdrafts are most commonly used to finance the day-to-day fluctuations in the operating working capital requirements. As such overdrafts will accommodate short-term outflows to finance payments to creditors and employees. Major capital expenditure requirements will usually be met by longer-term types of finance, the term of which will usually be calculated to match the useful economic life of the item in question.

The major drawbacks of overdrafts lie in the bank's right to foreclose at any time. This is a particular problem in circumstances where the company is not performing well and the bank is worried about its security. The other main problem arises when companies end up using an overdraft as a form of medium- or long-term finance. As a general principle it is better to finance short-term needs with short-term finance and long-term needs with long-term finance. This is because if a company is financing a long-term project of some sort it needs the security for planning purposes of knowing that the finance being utilised cannot be withdrawn until the end of the scheme by which time the company should have realised enough funds from the project to repay the borrowing. An example in the hotel trade would be the types of finance utilised to facilitate the building of an hotel. Typically a long-term loan secured upon the building with a schedule of repayments lasting perhaps twenty-five years or the expected life of the property will be used. To finance such a project through an overdraft facility would be both costly and would lead to insecurity during any difficult trading periods.

Most hotels, however, will think in terms of using term loan finance for their core debt arrangements, for the reasons described above. In arranging such facilities, the hotelier should pay particular attention to any covenants forming part of the loan documentation. It is becoming increasingly popular for term loan finance to include financial performance covenants (e.g. stipulating minimum interest cover ratios etc. throughout the life of the loan). Any breach of such limits will automatically create a condition of default, the effect of which is usually to make the loan repayable on demand. Care should always be taken therefore to ensure that financial performance covenants are set sufficiently comfortably to ensure that a small shortfall against budget does not take the company into breach.

Other types of short-term finance

There are numerous other forms of short-term financing instruments, many of which are very similar to each other. In the hotel sector certain of these have been increasingly used in recent years. The main categories are leasing and hire purchase. Leasing of assets and hire purchase are means of financing that suit certain aspects of hotel funding requirements. The general principle is that instead of tying up valuable capital which could otherwise be used as working capital to purchase assets such as furniture, fixtures and fittings, the company leases those assets from a finance company. In this way the company has merely to fund the rental payments on the asset rather than having to raise significantly more finance to purchase the asset in the first place. Usually such arrangements are timed to coincide with the expected lifetime of the asset. At the end of that time, depending upon the type of finance arrangement, the company usually either gains outright ownership of the asset in the case of a hire purchase scheme or continues to enjoy unlimited use of the asset in return for a continuing nominal rent during the secondary lease period.

Another variation upon the theme is where a company has already purchased an asset but wishes to release some of the capital that is tied up in it. In such circumstances the company could apply for a sale and leaseback scheme whereby it sells the asset to a finance company which then leases the asset back to the company in return for a rental income. In this way the company has released some capital via the sale of the asset, but continues to enjoy unlimited use of the asset.

Such funding instruments are particularly useful for companies that are not cash rich due to the relatively high rates of interest that are payable. However, hotels are major users of these methods of finance because they require a large quantity of assets that are ideally suited for financing by these means. Such assets include televisions, furniture and fittings, security systems, computing systems and so on. Like most other industries, the hotel sector also utilises these instruments to finance motor vehicles.

Other sources of finance

10.6   The chief sources of such finance, which usually comes in the form of grants or soft loans, are the UK Government, the EC, local government and a variety of agencies responsible for distributing grants. The availability of assistance is largely dependent upon location because most grants are allocated to either specific areas or to specific types of area. For the purposes of distributing grants and other aid the Government has divided the UK into Assisted and Non-Assisted areas. The assisted areas are further divided into Development and Intermediate areas. The areas are categorised according to levels of unemployment and economic growth or decline. As such the assisted areas are those which have experienced relative economic decline and have higher than average levels of unemployment. It is these areas in which both the Government and the EC concentrate their budgets for grants and other types of aid.

The hotel industry is often eligible for aid, especially where it can be demonstrated that a project generates employment and draws tourists and other guests in from other regions or from abroad. To achieve an award of a grant or other aid it is necessary first to discover if the particular project is eligible for aid. This can be done by contacting the local authority, the DTI, the Department of the Environment and the various EC institutions such as the European Regional Development Fund, as well as any other bodies which may operate in the area.

If a project is eligible the process involved in submitting an application for a grant is usually every bit as detailed as any commercial application, with a business plan and detailed financial forecasts required. Any aid granted will often be on the basis that the company must fulfil certain requirements, such as an undertaking to maintain a certain level of employment for a specified period.

There are some other forms of aid that can potentially benefit businesses even if they are not located in an Assisted area. These include the DTI loan guarantee scheme (see 10.5 above). This is applied for via whichever bank the company is negotiating with for a loan or overdraft scheme. The DTI also used to operate a nationwide scheme to contribute to the fees of management consultants. This has now ceased but the DTI still operates various similar local schemes in conjunction with local Chambers of Commerce and TECs. The aim of these schemes is to help companies meet the challenges of the Single Market and it is designed to concentrate on aspects such as marketing, planning and so on. It also involves an analysis of the current state of the business with a view to establishing the full potential of it.

Another scheme that hotels are well positioned to take advantage of is the current YT programme that places young people in temporary employment to gain practical experience and training. The benefit for an hotel is that this can be a source of cheap labour, with the added advantage of being able to recruit any outstanding candidates at the end of their placement. The costs of the scheme are low because the Government pays the trainee's weekly allowances. The employer's obligation is to provide sufficient work experience in order that the trainee may qualify for his National Vocational Qualifications level 2. This involves both on-the-job training and allowing the trainee time-off to attend college. There are some drawbacks to be considered, not least of which are the inherent problems involved in relying on untrained employees.

The possibility of achieving the award of a grant or some other form of aid is clearly worth investigating particularly if the project is located in an assisted area. This is particularly the case when the proposed hotel is part of a larger scheme to develop the tourist or conference trade of a particular area. It is worth bearing in mind, however, that most grants are awarded on the basis that the project will only have sufficient finance to proceed if the grant is awarded. In other words if the project already has all the financial backing that it needs then it is very unlikely to succeed in achieving the award of a grant.

Raising the finance

10.7   Raising the desired type of finance, once identified, is a complex, time-consuming business usually best delegated to specialist advisers. The process of how best to go about this is beyond the scope of this chapter. However, the starting point for just about all finance-raising is the production of an authoritative and persuasive business plan.

The business plan

10.8   The business plan is an important tool for assessing the value, as well as enabling management to focus on, the strategic objectives of the business. It can, for example, act as an indispensable validation in the calculation of how much finance is required. Given that such circumstances usually revolve around acquiring a hotel or company, the actual cost of acquisition is usually known. Whether that amount is too much depends upon a variety of factors.

The valuation, the acquirer's own cashflow projections, which will indicate whether or not the expected business generated can sustain the costs of financing the property, the reasonableness of the assumptions and the degree of risk attached to them all affect its value. The plan has to highlight these issues and support management's conclusions, clearly and coherently.

There is no denying that the preparation of a business plan can be a heavy burden, and may take some people into previously unchartered water. In such circumstances, it is often advisable to seek assistance from professional advisers such as accountants and/or consultants. But it is vital that management are heavily involved in the process and understand and agree with the key objectives and assumptions.

The typical processes which need to be performed in preparing a business plan is summarised opposite.

Summary

10.9   The key questions that the business plan is intended to answer are as follows.

(*a*)   Does the project have a realistic chance of being successful?

(*b*)   Has the research on the market and potential demand been thorough?

(*c*)   Is there a need for the product?

(*d*)   Does the management team have the appropriate skills and expertise?

(*e*)   Are the financial projections robust?

It is essential that the plan is structured in order to meet the requirements of the potential investors. However, it should be assumed that few, if any, potential investors who actually read the business plan will know anything about the proposed activity.

Example

Stage	Subjects covered
Information gathering	Potential and existing competitors Potential customers and likely demand Profile of your hotel(s) Profile of your company/group (if applicable) Profile of key members of the Board and/or Management Products Legislation affecting the hotel industry Any market research information considered relevant
Documenting the project	Description of the project, the site to be acquired, the development (if applicable) and its key stages, the products and services Photographs and drawings New technology Distinguishing features (e.g. how this hotel is different from its competitors) Key objectives Alternative uses
Documenting marketing information	Analysis of demand Analysis of customers Analysis of competitors – distance from our hotel – strengths and weaknesses of competitors Main marketing method Types of products Trends: locally and nationally Pricing strategy
Documenting the management and organisation structure	Management team, detailed CVs including background, professional qualifications, experience, key strengths **cont...**

Stage	Subjects covered
	Structure of senior management team Skills shortages (if any) plus steps for overcoming shortage Reporting structure Incentives, share options or profit sharing plans
Documenting financial projections	Forecasts of profit and loss, cash flow and balance sheets, typically for five years Monthly forecasts of the above, typically for two years and quarterly for following three years Key assumptions, plus supporting research Impact of key risks or uncertainties (sensitivity analyses) 'Worst case' sensitivity scenario Explanations of financial information, with key financial ratios
Documenting methods of finance	Equity injected by founders and management (where applicable and recent) Alternative private sources of equity or other finance (e.g. hire purchase) Public sector assistance (if any) Funding needs (plus why and when needed) Timing of funding Key financial controls and management reporting arrangements
Independent review of financial projections (optional)	Report by an independent consultant on reasonableness of assumptions

Chapter 11

Management

Introduction

11.1   The responsibility for the performance of an hotel rests ultimately with its manager. The issues involved in effective management are common to every type of business or organisation. This chapter therefore concentrates upon any issues that have particular importance in the hotel trade. Each hotel tends to serve a target market providing a certain level of service for a particular range of client. For whatever level of service that may be, the success or otherwise of the hotel will depend chiefly upon the manner and dedication with which the staff work to provide it. The manager's job can be reduced to two key components – ensuring that the staff do their jobs properly and taking key operating decisions. However, in order to examine the topic of management this chapter breaks it down into various segments starting with objectives.

Objectives

11.2   To manage any organisation effectively management must establish their objectives so there is a clear target to aim for and so that the performance can be monitored and compared with the objectives set. For an hotel the first clear objective should be to establish what kind of customer it should cater for and therefore the market it must aim to target. This has implications for the type of service provided and the facilities required. It will also affect all kinds of other considerations, including marketing objectives, staff recruitment and training and capital expenditure plans.

Beyond the overall objectives there are a number of other areas where the setting of objectives, whether formally or informally, will aid the manager in achieving best possible performance. Some of these can be specific targets for staff to achieve, others can be more general objectives such as creating a culture amongst staff that is loyal to the hotel and which is amenable to continuous improvement in the quality of service and general staff productivity.

Whatever the objective, it is important that it is achievable, stated clearly and is properly communicated to the relevant members of staff. If any of these conditions are not met the whole rationale behind objective setting will be lost and the exercise is likely to be a futile one. Finally, while objectives need to be set it is important that they always remain merely objectives and do not take on a significance of their own so that where necessary they can be adapted to suit the altered environment.

Planning

11.3   Planning focuses on looking at the future, identifying alternative courses of action and selecting preferred options. It also requires revisiting objectives that have been set in the past, evaluating achievement and redefining those objectives and the routes forward. Activities at all levels within an hotel should be planned, and the impact of any decision by one department assessed for all departments. For example, the type and timing of food offered by the restaurant may alter the types of customers booking accommodation in the hotel and therefore, the marketing strategies that should be followed. Communication within the hotel between managers and staff, and between departments must be developed. Planning is not just an activity at top management level. It should involve all employees. Objective setting does not operate in a vacuum. It requires information. A key element of planning will therefore be to identify what information is needed by the hotel to enable it to make decisions. The sorts of information required might include:

(*a*)   occupation levels;

(*b*)   profitability levels;

(*c*)   prices per room;

(*d*)   other services purchased, split by type;

(*e*)   seasonality data;

(*f*)   data on rival hotels.

From this data, forecasts can then be made on future outcomes which can assist the decision-making process.

Progress reviews

11.4   Once decisions are made, regular review of progress will need to be made. This can be shown diagrammatically as follows:

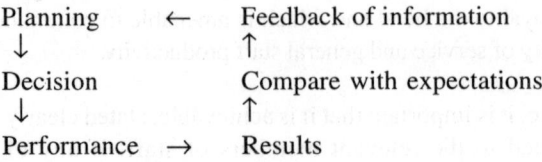

Planning   ←   Feedback of information
    ↓   ↑
Decision   Compare with expectations
    ↓   ↑
Performance   →   Results

However, monitoring needs to go further than just review the outcome of decisions made by management; it also needs to assess the well-being of the organisation generally, and provides the raw data to stimulate a decision-making process where concerns are identified. The best known formalised control system designed for this purpose is Budgetary Control.

Budget control

11.5   A typical process for devising the budget might be as follows:

(*a*)   set overall targets for sales, costs and profit targets;

(*b*)   divide these targets amongst the departments into initial targets;

(*c*)   discuss initial targets with managers responsible;

(*d*)   allow managers responsible to present alternatives/dispute assumptions and agree revisions; and

(*e*)   compile aggregate of revised budgets and reconcile to original company-wide plan. Repeat process if insufficient proximity.

Chapter 12

Marketing

Introduction

12.1   The aim of this chapter is to provide a broad overview of marketing and to give the reader prompts about the range of issues which can be considered when planning and implementing it.

In the space available this cannot be a complete and thorough analysis. There are many sources of further information and advice. At the end of the chapter we offer a directory of some organisations which might be able to help with information, training and other types of assistance.

What is marketing?

12.2   Marketing is a term which is regularly used by business people, customers and the media often in different contexts, often with different meanings. It is, perhaps, this variety of definitions which has led to confusion about marketing. Marketing is often used to refer to various activities including:

(*a*)   selling;

(*b*)   advertising;

(*c*)   promotional activity;

(*d*)   PR.

Each of the above represents the most visible aspects of marketing but does not give the whole picture. Key elements of marketing are reviewed later in this chapter. The Chartered Institute of Marketing's definition of marketing is:

> 'Marketing is the management process responsible for identifying, anticipating and satisfying customer requirements, profitably'.

In order to ensure the business is effective in exploiting customer needs, management will typically prepare a marketing strategy and action plan. This will often include, for example:

(i)   specific business/marketing objectives;

(ii)   a review of the market;

(iii)   specification of the product or service offered;

(iv)   a profile of its target customers and market sectors;

(v)   how the business will charge for its products and services;

(vi)   how new customers will be won and existing customers retained; and

(vii)   organisational responsibilities.

Understanding the market

12.3   Each business operates in a complex and dynamic environment. It is essential that management continually monitors the market place to ensure that opportunities are exploited and threats to the business are anticipated. The first component of marketing is thus understanding the market through research and analysis.

Below are key areas you may wish to address.

(*a*)   Competition – who are the competition; what services do they provide; what do they charge; who are their customers; how can we be different and better than them? Are other hotels our only competitors?

(*b*)   Customer segmentation – not all customers are the same. Do we want to target e.g. UK or international clients, business users, the short break sector or holidaymakers? Each will have different requirements and provide different business opportunities. Management must segment and prioritise the potential market.

(*c*)   'Environment' – the market place will be affected by changes in legislation, local politics, demography and the economy. Significant changes in the environment need to be anticipated and planned for.

Management's understanding of the market place and their hotel's positioning within it will be important in the development of a successful marketing plan.

You should undertake research on a regular basis to keep track of the market. This need not involve great expense. Information can be gained inexpensively from, e.g. published research, trade journals and other press; talking to clients; visiting competitors. It is advisable to develop a system for collecting and maintaining information. This can be as simple as a set of files which can be reviewed and analysed when needed.

The marketing mix

12.4   The marketing mix comprises the set of issues about which management can make choice and decisions to influence demand for their hotel. At the

12.5 *Marketing*

simplest level the marketing mix is encompassed by what are known as the 'Four Ps'.

(*a*)   Product – tangible features of product or service (e.g. size of rooms, location, facilities) and intangible benefits (e.g. convenience, hospitality, comfort).

(*b*)   Price – standard price; discounts and price promotions.

(*c*)   Place – the two elements of this are distribution channels (e.g. use of intermediaries to make your hotel more accessible to potential clients) and physical distribution issues such as location.

(*d*)   Promotion – different types of techniques (e.g. PR, advertising, direct mail).

Product

12.5   The two principal issues which need addressing when making decisions about your hotel product are:

(*a*)   offering a product which meets the physical and psychological needs and expectations of the target markets;

(*b*)   differentiating the offering from the competition.

Choices can be made which range from the physical facilities available (e.g. number of bedrooms; style and content of bedrooms; conference/business services; recreation amenities; and restaurants/menus) to the intangible elements of product such as quality of service, image and booking facilities. The hotel may wish to consider participating in a voluntary classification scheme (such as those run by the tourist boards).

Prices

12.6   It can be argued that pricing is the most powerful and important element of the marketing mix. It not only determines the level of income and profit (or loss), it can also influence perceptions about the hotel and its position in the market. Marketing decisions about price can be complex and difficult. With insufficient consideration, it is easy to make expensive mistakes. There are a wide variety of methods for calculating price. These include broadly the following.

(*a*)   Cost based – these techniques broadly relate to marking-up costs and break even analysis.

(*b*)   Profitability based – these techniques relate to the profit or income targets and calculation of the prices and occupancy levels needed to achieve these. Typical issues include ROCE (return on capital employed) and marginal pricing.

(*c*)   Market related – these issues include, amongst others, positioning relative to competitors; promotional pricing; loss leaders; image pricing;
and market price points.

Place

12.7   Place encompasses distribution in terms of physical distribution and
of distribution channels. At the most fundamental, physical distribution involves decisions being made about the location of an hotel. Site selection
criteria will depend on the markets you are targeting (see 4.7 above).

Distribution channels are the means of making your hotel accessible to clients
and potential clients. You have choices to make between either, or both of,
direct sales or the use of intermediaries. Potential intermediaries include, for
example:

(*a*)   clients;

(*b*)   travel agents;

(*c*)   tourist information centres;

(*d*)   incentive travel agencies;

(*e*)   tour operators;

(*f*)   purchasing functions in large organisations; and

(*g*)   special hotel reservation services.

The key disadvantage of using intermediaries is that it is usually necessary to
give them some of your profit margin in the form of commissions or discounts.
However, they give you more extensive coverage of the market, making your
hotel more accessible to clients.

Direct selling has a number of advantages including:

(i)   greater opportunity to develop a 'relationship' with your potential clients;

(ii)   more control over the type and quality of information;

(iii)   more scope for 'closing the sale'.

Promotion

12.8   The role of promotion is ultimately to develop some level of control
over the demand for an hotel. Promotion involves the communication of im-
ages and messages to specific audiences. Much time and money can be wasted
on promotional activity. In this section we suggest some guidelines to help
you to plan promotional activity which is effective and gives you a

reasonable return on your investment. We also provide a summary of some of the techniques which are available.

Planning

Some of the issues which you need to consider include the following.

(a)   Target audiences – define the groups of people or organisations to whom you need to communicate. These might include a variety of types of client; intermediaries and influencers (e.g. press).

(b)   Messages – confirm the messages you want to convey to each audience. Elements of the message usually include the hotel's USPs (Unique Selling Propositions) which differentiate from others in the market place.

(c)   Media – examine the full range and combinations of media which could target each audience.

(d)   Testing – before committing yourself to investing in a full programme of promotional activity, test the appropriateness and effectiveness of your messages and media.

(e)   Objectives – set measurable objectives for your promotional activity (e.g. number of enquiries; number of new clients; increased revenue and profit).

(f)   Monitoring – set up systems for monitoring the effectiveness of specific activities and campaigns. You will then be able to find out what works and what is a waste of money.

Potential techniques

The range of promotional techniques which are available is vast. A selection for you to consider are listed below:

  (i)   brochures;

 (ii)   advertising (press, TV, radio, posters);

(iii)   direct mail;

(iv)   public relations;

 (v)   press/media relations;

(vi)   telephone selling;

(vii)   personal selling (face-to-face);

(viii)   sales promotion (offering incentives);

(ix)   sponsorship;

 (x)   exhibitions; and

(xi)   trade fairs.

Client care

12.9   The performance of an hotel in the market place is heavily dependent upon the reputation it gains for the quality of service, hospitality and care provided to its clients. Management and staff are essential to delivering a high quality service. Clients will tend to remember the personal aspects of service (e.g. politeness, use of their names) rather than the physical or tangible aspects of the product. 'People' can be referred to as the 'fifth P' of the marketing mix. Ensuring effective and superior client care depends on the attitudes and motivation of staff. It is down to management to show what is required and to provide the tools and training to help staff achieve the standards. Some basic elements of client care which should be considered include:

(*a*)   telephone answering (speed, politeness, helpfulness, use of names etc.);

(*b*)   efficiency and speed of booking and check out;

(*c*)   use of clients' names;

(*d*)   tidiness and cleanliness (bedrooms, reception);

(*e*)   speed and accuracy of service (e.g. room service); and

(*f*)   staff who smile.

Client surveys

12.10   Client surveys are an essential tool for monitoring the performance of an hotel and for identifying opportunities to develop and enhance the product/service. Typical issues which surveys can address include the following.

(*a*)   Client satisfaction – a well-structured questionnaire can help monitor objectively levels of satisfaction generally and specific aspects of the service. The information gained can be used to set targets for monitoring performance.

(*b*)   Complaints – many people try to avoid the confrontation of making a verbal complaint. A survey can provide an easier means of complaining. Complaints are not to be feared. No hotel or its service is always perfect. Early identification of complaints gives the opportunity to put things right before the hotel's reputation is severely damaged.

(*c*)   Service developments – surveys can be used to identify changing client needs and their ideas for new or improved services.

Before initiating a survey, be sure of what its objectives are. Your objectives will help to decide on, for example, questions, samples and methodologies.

Techniques which can be used include the following.

Self-completion questionnaires

These can be left in rooms, given to people on checking out or posted to them at their home or business address. In order to ensure that they are completed correctly and a reasonable response rate is achieved, the following points should be considered.

(i) Design – have the questionnaire designed and printed to reflect the style and quality of the hotel. This need not be expensive and is another way of enhancing its image.

(ii) Test – before launching the questionnaire, test it on a selection of clients to check that the questions are clear and that they know how to complete it and return it. This will also give information about response rates which can be expected.

(iii) Confidentiality – response rates and the quality of the feedback are often improved if the respondents know that they can remain anonymous. Consider using an independent agency to receive and analyse responses and do not insist on respondents giving their names and addresses.

(iv) Response mechanisms – response rates can also be improved if it is made easy for people to return the questionnaires. Consider reply-paid envelopes or a special post box at reception.

(v) Incentives – offering incentives such as small gifts of entry into a prize draw, can dramatically increase response rates. Be careful that you have a large enough supply of the gifts as response rates can be over 80 per cent if the incentive is attractive enough. With prize draws, it is vital to take advice on relevant regulations.

Telephone surveys

These are probably best conducted shortly after clients have returned home or to the office. They have the advantage that the interviewer can probe more deeply the reasons for particular responses. Such surveys are probably best planned and performed by specialist independent researchers.

Discussion groups

Very useful information can be gained from organising discussion groups. A sample of customers is invited to attend a meeting which is chaired, usually, by an independent 'facilitator'. Incentives can be offered to encourage people to attend (e.g. a free dinner). Discussion groups aim to obtain an in-depth understanding of attitudes, perceptions and reasons behind changing needs.

Summary

12.11   When conducting a survey it is not usually practical to collect information from every member of the total relevant population. This can be very expensive; there is not just the cost of questionnaires, postage or telephone calls, for example, but also the cost of data processing and analysis. However, a good example of targeting the entire population, would be the placing of questionnaires in bedrooms: every guest has the opportunity to complete and return one. Accurate sampling is vital to obtaining information in which you can have confidence. It will be important to obtain advice on sampling from a research specialist. The specialist can advise on sample sizes and sampling techniques.

The frequency of client surveys will depend on what you want to know and how you will use the information. A continuous survey would for example, involve questionnaires in bedrooms; the data could be analysed on a monthly basis and performance indicators developed to be used to guide staff on what they are doing well or where the hotel needs to improve. At the other extreme, one-off surveys might be used to test the potential for a new service.

Management Letter Checklist

The following checklist gives examples of typical points that may be raised in an hotel management letter. The exact nature of the points, for each hotel, will obviously depend on the nature of the accounting system used and the quality of the internal controls operated by the hotel management. Further information on management letters is found in 5.19.

Account Area	Weakness Identified	Recommendation
Fixed assets	The fixed asset register does not reconcile to the nominal ledger.	A fixed asset reconciliation should be carried out on a regular basis.
	The fixed asset register has not been updated for all the additions and disposals in the period.	All movements of fixed assets should be recorded as soon as they occur.
	The depreciation charge was not calculated in accordance with the hotel's accounting policy.	Depreciation should be calculated in accordance with the hotel's stated policies.
Stock	No physical count of stock was carried out at the year end.	All stock must be counted at least once a year. It is usual, within the hotel industry, for a full count to be completed at the year end.
	No provision was made against old or damaged stock.	Although stock obsolescence is not a major problem for the hotel industry, staff should

Account Area	Weakness Identified	Recommendation
		provide against any old or damaged stock.
	Requisitions are carried out on an *ad hoc* basis, without authorisation by the department head.	Proper procedures should be laid down *re* the authorisation of stock requisitions and level of stock to be held.
Bank and cash	Bank reconciliations included a number of old items which had not been followed up.	All reconciling items should be cleared as soon as possible from the reconciliations.
	Some vouchers supporting petty cash payments were missing.	The cash office supervisor should ensure that all payments can be supported by authorised vouchers.
	There is no system of surprise checks of petty cash holdings by a member of staff independent of the cash function.	Surprise checks should be instituted to complement regular cash counts by cashier staff.
	The sales ledger does not reconcile to the nominal ledger.	Reconciliations between the main and sub ledgers should be carried out on a monthly basis.
	The sales ledger includes several overdue balances, due to poor credit control.	The sales ledger should be regularly reviewed and any overdue balances followed up with customers.
	Remittance advices from long stay customers are not retained.	All remittance advices should be kept, as a source of third party evidence.

Account Area	Weakness Identified	Recommendation
	Accrued income, *re* guests in residence at the year end, could not be reconciled to the reservations system.	The accrued income calculation should be reconciled to reservations and housekeeper's records.
	Some prepayments were not identified at the year end.	All purchase invoices should be reviewed on authorisation, and prepayments calculated as appropriate. Typical prepayments are telephone rental, maintenance contracts, laundry contracts etc.
Trade Debtors and Income	Discounts were given on room rates to guests, without proper authorisation.	All discounts should be authorised by the billing office manager or similar officer.
	Invoicing for banqueting and conference facilities, was often not completed until several weeks after the function took place.	All invoicing should be completed on a timely basis.
	Restaurant dockets were not used sequentially and no copy was kept by the kitchen department.	Checks should be made on the sequence of dockets and copies kept to ensure all meals are billed to guests.
Creditors and costs	Coin boxes are opened and the cash counted by one member of staff.	Two staff should be involved in the opening of boxes and the collection of cash. Receipts should be reconciled to the relevant telephone bill.

Account Area	Weakness Identified	Recommendation
	The purchases ledger does not reconcile to the nominal ledger.	Reconciliations between the main and sub ledgers should be carried out on a monthly basis.
	No reconciliations are carried out between purchase ledger balances and supplier statements.	Reconciliations should be carried out on a regular basis for all large creditor balances.
	Identification of accruals was not complete.	Accounts staff should review all invoices received after the year end for items relating to the prior year, and consider regular payments made in arrears, e.g. telephone, bank interest etc. They should also contact heads of other departments such as the housekeeper, bar manager etc. to identify any costs incurred not yet identified.
	There was evidence of duplicate payments occurring in the year.	All cheques awaiting signature should be accompanied by the relevant purchase invoices, which should then be stamped as paid.
	Not all purchase invoices are correctly authorised, agreeing prices and quantities received.	All invoices should be authorised by appropriate members of staff.
	Not all payments for entertainment etc. invoiced onto customers,	All payments should have supporting documentation.

Account Area	Weakness Identified	Recommendation
	could be supported by vouchers or invoices.	
Payroll costs	The payroll records do not reconcile to the nominal ledger.	Reconciliations should be carried out when making the payroll postings on a weekly or monthly basis.
	There are no standard contracts of employment issued to staff.	Standard terms and conditions should be issued to all staff.
	Timesheets for casual staff were not always authorised by their head of department before payment was made.	All timesheets should be authorised before wages are paid.
General points	The draft accounts did not comply with the *Companies Acts* and accounting standards.	All applicable standards should be followed in the preparation of financial statements.

Glossary

Audit exemption report

Report introduced to replace the audit requirement for companies with a turnover between £90,000 and £350,000.

Boarding-out costs

Costs faced by hotels who overbook guests and have to put them up at alternative hotels.

Bed and Breakfast (B&B)

Small establishments (except farmhouses) usually family run, offering comfortable accommodation at cheaper prices.

Generally provide accommodation, some services and breakfast, but no other meals.

Budget hotels

These are low cost hotels often operated by large chains. Accommodation is at a fixed price with standard accommodation and facilities throughout the chain.

Charge day

A period of 24 hours, starting from a constant arbitrary time (usually 12 pm), used in billing.

Country house hotels

Small hotels, usually personally run by the owners, offering civilised comfort, good service, and fine food, in an attractive and peaceful rural setting.

Most provide accommodation and breakfast and at least one other main meal and service to residents and non-residents without special contract.

Day lets

A non-overnight stay.

Dry sales

Sales of food.

Farmhouses

Covers both B&B and self-catering on a working farm. Accommodation types range from B&B in old farmhouses, modern bungalows and tied cottages to self-catering in converted barns, oast houses, old buildings and stables, plus all of the above B&B ranges. The majority offer evening meals and most meals will incorporate either local or home produce.

Fidelity income

A bond covering all cashiers, all employees handling cash and those in charge of safe-deposit boxes.

Guesthouses and private hotels

Establishments which provide accommodation and breakfast and at least one other main meal and service for residents only.

Hotels

Establishments which provide accommodation and breakfast and in most cases at least one other main meal and service to residents and non-residents without special contract. Note that many city-centre hotels may only provide bed and breakfast.

Housekeeper's report

Register of rooms occupied, kept by the housekeeper, which can be reconciled to the reservations system.

Inns

Generally small establishments other than hotels and motels, licensed for the sale of alcoholic liquor, having a bar open to members of the public and providing accommodation and breakfast and often other meals and/or bar food. Usually of historical interest offering comfortable accommodation. Often reflecting the area, they are situated in the centre of the local community.

Link man insurance

Insurance whereby commissionaires, porters and bell boys can drive guests' cars into and out of car parks.

Lodges

Name often given to budget hotels operated by large hotel chains. See budget hotels.

Motels and motor lodges

Establishments catering mainly for the motorist with parking for each bedroom/accommodation unit, and which may or may not provide meals. Motor lodges are most often next to a motorway/roadside restaurant and offer functional bedrooms with private facilities at reasonable prices.

Pre-opening expenses

Costs incurred before trading commences but not including formation expenses or deferred revenue expenditure.

Qualifying hotels

Accommodation which:

(*a*) is in a building of permanent nature;
(*b*) open for four or more months in the period April to October;
(*c*) has ten or more private bedrooms available to the public which are not normally in occupation for more than one month;
(*d*) provides services including the provision of breakfast and evening meals, the making of beds and cleaning of rooms.

Service charges	A charge levied on top of the sales price to be paid to the staff.
Soft opening	A rehearsed opening with complementary guests invited to use the services at nominal charge or for free.
Tips/Gratuities	A voluntary contribution by customers to reward staff for good service.
Tronc committee	A system by which service charges and gratuities are pooled and allocated to staff.
Tronc Master	Employee operating the tronc system.
Tronc system	The system whereby gratuities and service charges are paid to a central collection point. They are paid out by one member of staff the (Tronc Master) to the staff who earned them.
Walk outs	Guests who walk out without settling their bills.
Wet sales	Sales of beverages including alcohol.

Appendix 3

Useful Addresses

Association of British Travel Agents (ABTA)
55 Newman Street
London W1P 4AH
Telephone: 0171 637 2444

Association of Independent Tour Operators (AITO)
133a St Margaret's Road
Twickenham TW1 1RG
Telephone: 0181 744 9280

Automobile Association (AA)
Hotels Department
Floor 1, City Wall House
Basingstoke
Hampshire RG21 2HG
Telephone: 01256 20123

British Incoming Tour Operators Association (BITOA)
120 Wilton Road
London SW1V 1JZ
Telephone: 0171 931 0601

British Tourist Authority
Thames Tower
Black's Road
Hammersmith
London W6 9EL
Telephone: 0181 846 9000

Chartered Institute of Marketing
Moor Hall
Cookham
Maidenhead, Berks SL6 9QH
Telephone: 01628 524922
English Tourist Board

Thames Tower
Blacks Road
Hammersmith
London W6 9EL
Telephone: 0181 846 9000

Department of Environment (DoE)
2 Marsham Street
London SW1P 3EB
Telephone: 0171 276 0900

Department of Trade and Industry (DTI)
Ashdown House
123 Victoria Street
London SW1E 6RB
Telephone: 0171 215 5000

Hotel Catering and Institutional Management
Association (HCIMA)
191 Trinity Road
London SW17 7HN
Telephone: 0181 672 4251

Hotel and Catering Training Company (HCTC)
International House
7 High Street
Ealing W5 5DB
Telephone: 0181 579 2400

Institute of Public Relations
The Old Trading House
15 Northburgh Street
London EC1V OPR
Telephone: 0171 253 5151

London Tourist Board
26 Grosvenor Gardens
London SW1W ODU
Telephone: 0171 730 3450

Market Research Society
15 Northburgh Street
London EC1V OAH
Telephone: 0171 490 4911

RAC Enterprises Limited
PO Box 100
RAC House
Bartlett Street
Croydon
Surrey CR2 6XW
Telephone: 0181 686 0088

Scottish Tourist Board
23 Ravelston Terrace
Edinburgh EH4 3EU
Telephone: 0131 332 2433

Welsh Tourist Board
Brunel House
No 2 Fitzalan Road
Cardiff CF2 1UY
Telephone: 01222 499909

Index

TAXATION PUBLICATIONS

Tax Reference Annuals

Tolley's Income Tax 1995-96 £32.95

Tolley's Corporation Tax 1995-96 £28.95

Tolley's Capital Gains Tax 1995-96 £29.95

Tolley's Inheritance Tax 1995-96 £25.95

Tolley's Value Added Tax 1995-96 £28.95

Tolley's National Insurance Contributions 1995-96 £33.95

Tolley's Looseleaf Tax Services

Tolley's Tax Service (Income Tax, Corporation Tax and Capital Gains Tax) (4 volumes) £450.00

Tolley's VAT Service £325.00 (2 volumes)

Tolley's Inheritance Tax Service £120.00

Tax Periodicals

Tolley's Practical Tax £113 p.a.

Taxation £107 p.a.

Tolley's National Insurance Brief £132 p.a.

Tax Sources

Tolley's Official Tax Statements 1995-96 £39.95

Tolley's Tax Tables 1996-97 £12.95

Tolley's Tax Data 1995-96 £16.95

Tolley's Tax Cases 1995 £32.95

Tolley's Tax Office Directory 1996 £9.95

Tax Planning

Tolley's Tax Planning 1995-96 £69.50 (2 volumes)

Tolley's Estate Planning 1995-96 £34.95

Tolley's Tax Planning for Family Companies £tba

Tolley's Tax Planning for Private Residences £35.95

Tolley's Tax Planning for Post-Death Variations £36.95

Tolley's Adviser's Guide to Investment Planning 1995-96 £tba

Tax Compliance

Tolley's Tax Compliance and Investigations £tba

General Tax Guides

Tolley's Guide to Self-Assessment for the Self-Employed £16.95

Tolley's Guide to Self-Assessment for Employers and Employees £16.95

Tolley's Accounting Principles for Tax Purposes £36.95

Tolley's Self-Assessment £35.95

Tolley's Tax Guide 1995-96 £24.95

Specialist Tax Guides

Tolley's Anti-Avoidance Provisions £52.50

Tolley's Taxation of Lloyds Underwriters £55.00

Tolley's Taxation in Corporate Insolvency £tba

Tolley's Taxation of Foreign Exchange Gains and Losses £49.95

Tolley's Property Taxes 1995-96 £36.95

Tolley's Stamp Duties and Stamp Duty Reserve Tax £29.95

Tolley's Purchase and Sale of a Private Company's Shares £34.95

Tolley's UK Taxation of Trusts £37.95

Business Tax

Tolley's Schedule D £tba

Tolley's Capital Allowances 1995-96 £31.95

Tolley's Roll-over, Hold-over and Retirement Reliefs £39.95

Tolley's Partnership Taxation £tba

Employee Taxation

Tolley's Taxation of Employments £34.95

Tolley's Practical Guide to Employees' Share Schemes £36.95

Tolley's Pay and Benefits Handbook £23.95

Value Added Tax

Tolley's VAT Planning 1995-96 £34.95

Tolley's Practical VAT (Newsletter) £103 p.a.

Tolley's VAT Cases 1995 £60.00

Tolley's VAT on Construction, Land and Property £29.95

Tolley's VAT and Customs Appeals £tba

Tolley's VAT and Retailers £tba

Tolley's VAT in Europe £34.95

Tolley's VAT and the Partial Exemption Rules £tba

Tax Computations

Tolley's Tax Computations 1995-96 £35.95

Tolley's Taxwise I 1995-96 £26.95

Tolley's Taxwise II 1995-96 £25.95

Overseas Tax

Tolley's International Tax Planning £99.50

Tolley's Tax Havens £54.50

Tolley's Taxation of Offshore Trusts and Funds £49.50

Tolley's Taxation in the Republic of Ireland 1995-96 £29.95

Tolley's Taxation in the Channel Islands and Isle of Man 1995-96 £29.95

Tolley Tax books
Please list the titles that you require on the form below:

Title	No. of copies	Price	Amount £
Total £			

SIGNATURE _____ Date _____

Surname _____

Initials _____ Title (Mr, Mrs, Miss, Ms) _____

Job Title _____ Telephone _____

Full Name of Firm *(if applicable)* _____

Address _____

_____

_____ Postcode _____

Type of Organisation/Business _____

Number of Employees A ❏ 1-5 B ❏ 6-50 C ❏ 51-200 D ❏ 201-1000 E ❏ 1000+

Registered No.729731 England   VAT Registered No.243 3583 67

Tolley

A114

Please tick to request further information
Tolley Catalogue 1995-96 ❏
Details of Tolley Conferences ❏
Details of Client Marketing Services ❏

CHOICE OF PAYMENT METHOD:

Cheque enclosed £

Please make cheques payable to:
Tolley Publishing Company Ltd.

Please debit Tolley/Access/Visa† Account No.

† *Please delete as necessary*

Expiry Date

/
Month   Year

Please enter name and address of cardholder

Name _____

Address _____

_____

_____ Postcode _____

If you have a Tolley Account but have chosen to pay by cheque, Access or Visa please enter your Tolley Account Number to help us process your order

Tolley's
Tax Reference Annuals
1995-96

With each new edition the standard of excellence established in **Tolley's Tax Reference Annuals** over the past seventy-nine years is not simply maintained but consistently improved. Every year our experienced in-house authors edit and revise the annuals to ensure that you have the most up-to-date tax commentary available. This year, following extensive market research, major changes and improvements have been made to the 1995-96 editions:

- More than 200 additional worked examples
- Expanded to include references to the Inland Revenue's Internal Guidance Manuals for the first time
- Inclusion of newly reported Special Commissioners' decisions
- Improved indexes
- A complete overhaul of the VAT annual to take account of the VAT Act 1994

The collective result is a concise set of reference works expressly designed to keep the user fully up-to-date with the minimum of effort.

Tolley's Income Tax 1995-96
Glyn Saunders MA, David Smailes FCA

July 1995	950pp approx	**Order Code IT95**
ISBN 1 86012 008-3		**£32.95**

Tolley's Corporation Tax 1995-96
Glyn Saunders MA, Alan Dolton MA(Oxon)

July 1995	550pp approx	**Order Code CT95**
ISBN 1 86012 011-3		**£28.95**

Tolley's Capital Gains Tax 1995-96
Patrick Noakes MA FCA ATII, Gary B Mackley-Smith FFA FIAB AIMgt

July 1995	650pp approx	**Order Code CGT95**
ISBN 1 86012 010-5		**£29.95**

Tolley's Inheritance Tax 1995-96
Patrick Noakes MA FCA ATII, Jon Golding ATT

July 1995	300pp approx	**Order Code IHT95**
ISBN 1 86012 009-1		**£25.95**

Tolley's Value Added Tax 1995-96
Robert Wareham BSc(Econ) FCA

July 1995	760pp approx	**Order Code VAT95**
ISBN 1 86012 012-1		**£28.95**

Tolley's National Insurance Contributions 1995-96
From an original text by Neil D Booth FCA FTII
Edited by Jon Golding ATT with consulting editors, KPMG, Employee Issues Group Leeds

June 1995	500pp approx	**Order Code NIC95**
ISBN 1 86012 013-X		**£33.95**

─────────────── **ORDERS AND ENQUIRIES** ───────────────

To Tolley's Customer Services Department at Tolley Publishing Co. Ltd., FREEPOST, 2 Addiscombe Road, Croydon, Surrey, CR9 5WZ.
Telephone: 0181-686 9141 Fax: 0181-686 3155.

Tolley

Remember, all Tolley publications are available on 21 days' approval.